HOW TO GROW TALL
POPPIES

A PRACTICAL GUIDE TO CULTIVATING
HIGH-PERFORMANCE TEAMS

RAJIV JAYARAJAH

How to Grow Tall Poppies
A PRACTICAL GUIDE TO CULTIVATING HIGH-PERFORMANCE TEAMS
Rajiv Jayarajah

Bare Inc.
Australia
www.bareinc.com.au
email: rajiv@bareinc.com.au

Copyright © 2020 Rajiv Jayarajah

ISBN 978-0-6489273-0-3 (paperback)

All rights reserved.

No part of this publication may be reproduced, distributed or transmitted in any form or by any means, including photocopying, recording, or other electronic or mechanical methods, without the prior written permission of the publisher, except in the case of brief quotations embodied in critical reviews and certain other non-commercial uses permitted by copyright law. For permission requests, write to the publisher, addressed "Attention: Permissions Coordinator," at the address above.

Author: Rajiv Jayarajah
Editor: Nikki M Group Pty Ltd
Cover Design: BookDesignTemplates.com
Book Layout: thesqueezebox.com.au

Printed by IngramSpark

How to grow tall poppies/ Jayarajah R. —1st ed.

Dedicated to my beautiful wife and my son.
Every day your love makes me strive to be a better man.

CONTENTS

Preface	7
Introduction	13
PART I: BARRIERS TO HIGH PERFORMANCE	**17**
Defining High Performance	19
Three Hard Truths	27
A New Way Forward	33
PART II: THE HIGH-PERFORMANCE TEAM MODEL	**41**
Trait 1 – Trust	45
Trait 2 – Respect	59
Trait 3 – Purpose	73
Trait 4 – Accountability	91
Trait 5 – Open Communication	119
Trait 6 – Strategic Flexibility	137
Trait 7 – Empowerment	147
PART III: ACHIEVING HIGH PERFORMANCE	**163**
Implementing the High-Performance Team Model	165
Conclusion	181
Acknowledgements	183
References	185

PREFACE

As long as I can remember, I have been fascinated by human behaviour and business. Throughout my childhood and teenage years, my Dad travelled the globe to expand our food business. One of his favourite programs to watch on TV was Business Sunday. Knowing this, I would get up early and watch it with him. Not understanding most of the concepts, Dad guided my knowledge on business, which included an explanation on how people's behaviour and actions led to different outcomes – good and bad – and that this could affect the performance of a business.

As I grew up, my fascination with how people behaved had morphed into a curiosity around why people within the same group act differently. I decided to study for a Bachelor of Arts in Criminology and Sociology at the University of Melbourne. From there, I went straight into pursuing a business degree and was accepted into The Master of Applied Commerce at the University of Melbourne. It was here that I was able to combine my understanding of human behaviour with business, in the form of marketing. This led me to a career developing and leading high-performance teams across the banking, energy and technology sectors.

I regularly read about leadership and leaders and was always striving to improve myself and build my team's capability. In my first leadership role, there was no handbook on how to lead and drive performance. Instead, I had to rely on what I had learned to date and when unsure, wing it. *Failure is a great teacher.*

My biggest lessons came from having to let people go due to poor performance and making people redundant due to changes in a company's structure. In these situations, I would ask myself what I could have done differently and what they could have done differently to change the outcome.

However, my hardest lessons came from dealing with senior leaders whom I felt had a toxic approach to management: using fear, intimidation, and ridicule to drive short-term performance gains. Then, came the statement that changed everything...

"Raj, the reason you are not feeling fulfilled is that you are not following your passion, which is to develop people." I stared blankly at my psychologist. After spending hours discussing my marketing career, her most significant insight was that I needed to leave that behind and focus on developing people. Did I hear that correctly?

At the time, my mind could not comprehend the thought of leaving a successful career to start over again. Change is scary: Why follow your heart, when you can play it safe? I wondered if it was possible to have a career that focused on developing the people that make up the business. Faced with such enormous change, I acted. I landed a senior marketing role in a leading technology company. Though, in the back of my mind, I kept coming back to the idea of developing leaders.

Borrowing from an old Chinese proverb, my father used to say to me, "When the wind blows hard, you have two choices: build a windbreak and pray it holds, or build a windmill and harness its energy."

Three years ago, I decided to leave the corporate life and step into the tornado of running my own business. I chose to focus on developing high performance leaders and teams. I started *Bare*

Coaching on the philosophy of stripping back complex leadership challenges and laying bare an actionable path forward to positive results. I wanted to support leaders to rise up to become more inspiring, authentic leaders and thus, have the skills, insight and knowledge to create their high-performance teams. I wrote this book to provide every leader – experienced or new – with a practical guide on how to drive performance by building their windmill and harnessing the energy of every member of their team.

My book, *How to Grow Tall Poppies*, is not about how one person can grow tall and stand out from the rest, but how a whole team can strive to achieve common goals within a business to grow tall and strong.

In the following pages, you will be guided to develop new strategies and mindsets to help your teams and thus, your business to grow tall and stand out from the competition. Great leaders do not rise on the hard work of others. They raise others up through their own hard work.

Rajiv Jayarajah

> "Coming together is a beginning; keeping together is progress; working together is success."
> — Henry Ford

INTRODUCTION

Have you ever laid awake at night, unable to sleep because of the endless thoughts of work crashing through your mind like a runaway train?

I know I have many times throughout my career. My approach to dealing with ever-consuming thoughts was to write them down on paper: a giant to-do list. However, the peace of mind was temporary. Like a deep-sea explorer, the deeper I went, the more darkness and less treasure I saw.

Underlying my general anxiety was the sensation that I was not the leader I wanted to be. Specifically, I was not the leader that inspired my team to step up and do their best. Not because I told them to, but because they wanted to.

I had built my career on being able to see around corners – I identified problems others could not and put in place strategies to prevent them. My job was to make sure that the train carrying our results stayed on track no matter what, and I was good at it too.

> **"THE IRONY WAS THAT I NEVER FORESAW MY TRAIN DERAILING."**

It was a Wednesday night. I had put my 3-year-old son to bed and was packing for a flight the next morning. I had a great job with a dream company and a fantastic team. I had recently been tapped on the shoulder to turn around a fledgling start-up business. I had a meeting scheduled with the CEO to provide an updated on my progress the next morning. Since taking over, I was turning around their business' performance. The train was slowly leaving the station.

Unlike the movies, my life-changing moment did not come with bright lights, explosions or music. It was subtle, starting with a build-up of pressure in my chest; almost like indigestion. When the tingling began in my left arm, I knew something was not right. I told my wife to call an ambulance. Within minutes, the paramedics had arrived and very quickly swung into action.

My world was changing around me, except I refused to believe it. Searching for answers, I asked the paramedic how long this would take because I had a flight to catch tomorrow. Wrong question! He looked at me in utter disbelief and then said in a calm, reassuring voice, "We're going as quickly as possible to the emergency room. You hang in there and try to relax." I think he assumed I was in shock – maybe I was – but I was also genuinely concerned I would miss my business flight. You see, at that time, I was of the thought that high-performance leader's like me did not let anything get in the way of their ambitions.

While waiting in the emergency room, I did not experience a life-changing montage of images going through my mind. Instead, my mind flickered between two trains of thought: family and work. Yes, I was wondering what life would be like for my wife and young son if I were no longer around, but admittedly, at this dire time, I was also thinking about what I needed to do at work. My mind was in complete conflict.

One part was trying to break through and tell me how dangerous the situation was. The other was in hyperdrive, compartmentalising the fear so that I could focus on the task at hand: getting out of the hospital and onto a plane tomorrow morning. Like a caged beast, the seriousness of the situation broke through my mental haze.

I pulled out my phone and wrote two vital messages — one to my wife and the other to my son — expressing to them how much I loved them and that I was sorry that I had let work consume the best of me. My time had come, and I was ashamed to say that they did not get the best of me — my career did.

After a long, anxious wait with doctors and surgeons, and after numerous scans and test, I was able to avoid heart surgery. The doctors discovered a treatable heart condition which did not require surgery. However, given my resting heart rate was sitting at around 110 bpm, I was ordered to have ten days forced medical leave.

Those ten days were hard — like an addict who had gone cold turkey. I had tied my identity and self-worth to being a high-performance leader, and now I felt lost. I was at a point where my mind was at work, regardless of my physical presence. Of course, I should not have worried; my team stepped up in my absence. But the assumption that I *had* to be on the job at all times to be successful had become ingrained. I always assumed that high-performance was a beast, and the beast demanded my sacrifice. That sacrifice was mental, physical, and spiritual in terms of the lack of time I had with my family. The biggest irony was that I convinced myself I was doing all of this to support my family.

Did I learn from this near-death experience? Well, no, not immediately. While still on medical leave, I receive a request from the executive to come back and take on a new priority project. Like an addict looking for their next fix, I jumped at the opportunity.

My train derailed...but I was able to learn from it and adapt how I worked to achieve greater efficiency. I did this by focusing on my team: creating a work culture where every team member was supported in an environment conducive to high-performance. I became the leader I wanted to be.

I believe we spend too much of our time at work not to be happy and inspired. Too many great aspiring leaders do not back themselves to take on more significant leadership roles because they feel they are not ready.

I want you to take the collective wisdom of what I have learnt, and from all the people I have interviewed and incorporated it into your leadership. I want you to understand and believe that change comes when everyone in the organisation makes the active choice to stretch themselves a little further and, in turn, lift their performance to greater heights.

> **"However, the change will only come when your team sees you, their leader, choosing and striving every day to create an environment where high performance can thrive."**

There are no fads or buzzwords in this book. I suspect you are looking for substance. I wrote it for people who genuinely believe they can have a positive impact, both on their business and on the people who choose to follow them—their teams. It does not matter if you are leading a team of 1 or 100, the foundations of high performance are the same.

I hope that as you read this book, you will begin to implement the changes outlined here. You will learn that to create a high-performance team, you do not need fancy perks or to be an established brand. There are companies out there achieving great things daily through their people, and I want you to become one of them. I did not say it would be easy, but together we can make sure it is not hard.

May this be the first step on your journey to becoming the high-performance leader the world needs.

PART 1

BARRIERS TO HIGH PERFORMANCE

Chapter 1

DEFINING HIGH PERFORMANCE

My first job after graduating was as a Marketing Product Manager with a top 4 bank. The banking culture was high stress and high reward. The graduate program felt like it took my natural desire to win and sharpened it into a weapon. It was in this environment that I had my first real taste of leadership and experienced terrible management. I learnt that a manager focuses on people's work output. A leader, however, inspires people to go above and beyond what they thought was possible and guides them to a higher state of engagement, drive, ability and purpose.

> **"I HAD THE PLEASURE OF WORKING FOR SOME TRULY INSPIRATIONAL AND REMARKABLE LEADERS, WHERE I GAVE IT MY ALL AND LOVED IT."**

There were long days and weekends filled with work. There was laughter, tears, highs and lows. But the consistent feeling was that we were in it together and were all driving towards a shared goal. It filled me with a joy, a sense of purpose and accomplishment.

I have also had the displeasure of working for some terrible managers who used fear, intimidation and public humiliation as tools to drive performance and feed their insecurities. My worst manager regularly ridiculed my work, and one day kept slamming her finger into my chest while yelling that I am stupid. The irony was that before she started, I had consistently ranked in the top 20% of managers under their performance ranking system. The second incident happened when I was more senior in my career. My male manager called me in for a meeting because I had taken a day of sick leave. The tensions in the meeting escalated, and he began yelling and slamming the table because he was not getting what he wanted. Unfortunately, neither of these incidents were isolated, and other people in the organisation had to put up with this terrible behaviour too.

The underlying message here is that any manager can use fear and intimidation to make people perform a task. However, it takes a leader to create a desire in people to perform at a high level consistently.

ARE YOU A LEADER OR A MANAGER?

At this point, you might be wondering which category you fit into: a manager or a leader. The fact that you are asking yourself this question is a good sign that you fit into the leadership category, or – at least – would like to. You see, good leaders are always questioning themselves and those around them, to grow.

A leader can understand the goals of a project and know how to guide their team to achieving those goals successfully. Their role is to create an environment of trust and respect through open communication. They encourage innovation, use insight when delegating tasks, and motivate their team. Leaders understand diversity, know the talents and skills of each team member, and can foster accountability. They also have flexible strategies to grow relationships, engage team members and to manage and resolve conflict.

> **"LEADERSHIP IS LIFTING A PERSON'S VISION TO HIGH SIGHTS, THE RAISING OF A PERSON'S PERFORMANCE TO A HIGHER STANDARD, THE BUILDING OF A PERSONALITY BEYOND ITS NORMAL LIMITATIONS."**
>
> — PETER F. DRUCKER

A leader will apply strategies to achieve the required outcomes, but how do they know if their strategies have been successful? How will *you* know if *your* team is successful? To do this, you need to define what high performance looks like in your business and how it can be measured.

WHAT IS 'HIGH PERFORMANCE' AND HOW IS IT MEASURED?

High performance has a different meaning in different industries, different companies and different people. High performance can also take on a different meaning for different teams within the same company. It is important to understand what high performance means to you and to have the understanding that this definition can change, develop and evolve.

Let me start by defining high performance in my terms.

As a leader, I always aim to have my team delivering results that have had them challenged and learning, and leaving them with a sense of fulfilment that they did the best they could do. Most importantly, I want them to be able to achieve these conditions consistently. It might surprise you to know that delivering consistently means I have to ensure my team are never operating at 100% all the time, as this could lead to burnout.

Take time now to reflect on how you define high performance. The table of key terms below may help you formulate your definition. Do you focus on the results *and* your team's development?

Key terms for high performance	
• highly skilled and talented	• collaboration
• goal focused	• healthy conflict and resolution
• produce superior results	• interchangeable roles
• innovative	• sense of accountability
• positive attitude	• high levels of trust
• clear sense of purpose	• open communications
• empowered	• flexible approach

My definition of high performance is ...

_____
_____
_____
_____
_____
_____
_____
_____
_____
_____
_____
_____

CASE STUDY
WHY YOUR CHOICE OF METRICS MATTERS

High performance is relative and individual for each leader. Let me illustrate this idea with an example from the fitness world.

Tim and Zoe train together at the gym. A typical measure of strength most lifters use is the concept of a one-repetition maximum (1RM). The one-repetition maximum is the heaviest a person can lift for a specific exercise one time. Let's say Tim can lift 150 kg and Zoe can lift 120 kg.

Relative to each other, one may assume that Tim is a higher performer (can lift more) than Zoe.

However, a way to even the playing field, and make this a relative measure of performance, is to divide the amount lifted by the person's weight. Let us assume Tim's weight is 96 kg and Zoe's weight is 70 kg. Using their power to weight ratio as the new benchmark for high performance, Tim can lift 1.56 times his body weight, whereas Zoe can lift 1.7 times her body weight (Table 1). Therefore, Zoe is proportionally stronger, hence a higher performer.

Table 1. Power to weight ratio

Metric	Tim	Zoe	Highest performer
One-repetition maximum	150 kg	120 kg	Tim
Power to Weight Ratio $= \frac{\text{amount lifted}}{\text{bodyweight}}$	150 ÷ 96 = 1.56	120 ÷ 70 = 1.71	Zoe

Take a moment and think about the measures you use to track the performance of your team. Now, consider how easily you can benchmark these measures across the team, organisation and competitors.

Key performance metrics and benchmarking

Measure	Can it be benchmarked across...		
	Team	Business	Industry
Example: Customer satisfaction score	No	Yes	Yes

Once you have found these measures, this can become a tangible way you can measure and track high performance over time. However, you also need to consider what metrics you will use to track the well-being and professional development of your team.

IDENTIFYING AREAS FOR IMPROVING PERFORMANCE

When wanting to improve performance, a leader usually has two areas in their control: business strategy and the capability of their people.

Business strategy
This could apply to your team or the business, depending on your level in the organisation. For example, you may focus on the business' resources and efforts on winning a specific type of customer or developing new products or services to improve the profitability of the company. One case which demonstrates the success of improving performance through changes to a business strategy is General Electric (GE). Jack Welch, a highly-regarded corporate leader, spent two decades as GE's chairman and chief executive, from 1981 to 2001. A chemical engineer by training, Welch transformed the company from a maker of appliances and light bulbs into an industrial and financial services powerhouse. During his tenure, GE's revenue grew nearly fivefold, and the firm's market capitalization increased thirtyfold.

Your people's capability
This involves understanding what your team is currently capable of achieving. Once you have a baseline, then increasing the team's strengths – either through ongoing training and development or recruiting specific skills and talents into the team – is a means of improving the overall performance of the team.

Most leaders focus on the first area – developing a great strategy. A clear business strategy is incredibly important, but for a strategy to be successful, your people need to be capable. People's capability tends to be handled by the annual performance reviews or another form of benchmarking which gives the leader a gauge of their team's skills.

It seems crazy that more time is often spent on developing strategies and plans, rather than on people's ability to execute the plan. Given that people are such a high cost of doing business, it makes sense that, as a leader, you spend time growing and developing your people.

A typical approach in most organisations is to rank all employees, and then focus on the top performers, the 10-20% of the organisation that is performing above average. Some leaders focus on the bottom 10% – people who are seen to be dragging down performance. They hope that removing poor performance will drive improvement across the organisation. Despite this, the same issues arise. This is because the strategy is either executed slowly or not effectively.

In Chapter 2, we will unravel why you might not be seeing the results you were hoping for using the traditional approach to performance and leadership. Pre-warning: some of these truths might be a bitter pill to swallow...but it will help you understand that by refocusing your energy, you can create a high-performance business and team.

Chapter 2

THREE HARD TRUTHS

I have worked in places that had all the great perks: free coffee, car parking, fancy lunches and all the newest technology. I have also worked in companies that ran on the smell of an oily rag, living with the fear that their business unit might be shut down tomorrow. What struck me was that the leaders in both of these environments had managed to achieve the extraordinary. They had delivered stellar results in terms of revenue and profits, but also managed to maintain high levels of staff happiness and performance. Their staff were inspired by them and wanted to go above and beyond.

Now, I was in these environments when new leaders took over. The performance dropped, staff morale plummeted, and the culture turned distrustful and sometimes toxic. This deterioration made me realise that free coffee and lunches cannot cover up for bad leadership; these perks were not the reason why people thrived.

After speaking with over 500 leaders and high-performance teams, it became apparent that three common barriers prevented high performance. These barriers existed across different industries and company sizes. However, it was clear that some leaders were aware of these barriers and were able to overcome them, while others in the same business could not.

1. YOU LEAD A GROUP OF PEOPLE, NOT A TEAM

What is the difference you ask? Let me explain.

It is common for us to define a specific group of people at work as a team, for example: the human resources team, the marketing team, the sales team. If only it were that easy. The critical difference between a group and a team is that a team has a shared goal, and a group does not. If you scratch the surface of most of these 'teams', you will quickly realise that they are each working individually towards their own goals. Whether that goal is a project or their next promotion, they are not bound by a common goal or purpose. It is the common goal and shared sense of purpose that creates a strong bond among the individuals and leads to a team that is motivated to perform at a high level.

I want you to ponder for a minute: would you categorise the people you lead as a group or a team? Use the descriptions below.

Group	Team
• connected through an interest or activity • do not share a common goal • specific roles or duties are not assigned to individuals • members work independently • members may not know each other	• shared or defined leadership • share a common goal • specific tasks or duties assigned to each individual • members are interdependent • members know each other's strengths and weaknesses

If you decide that the people you lead are a group, then do not stress – this book will help you bring them together into a high-performance team. If you decide that you are leading a team, then it is time to stare down the next hard truth.

2. YOUR STRATEGY IS INEFFECTIVE

I say this because, for a strategy to be hugely successful, it needs to be well-executed and achieve the desired outcomes. Think about the last plan you developed for your business. Did it achieve the desired result? If yes, great. Consider how the result was achieved: was it the team, the strategies, or luck? If no, what got in the way?

When I ask my clients, 'what got in the way?' the typical response is lack of time to think strategically. Top management spends less than three hours a month discussing strategy issues or making strategic decisions.

A study revealed that as much as 80% of senior management's time is devoted to problems that account for less than 20% of a company's long-term value. (Mankins, 2004).

Is this how you spend your time?

People assume that by creating a strategy, it will automatically translate into a high performance business. It will not. Your strategy might contain much brainpower that went into creating it, yet it will fall over at the point of execution. Why? Because people in the business execute the plan, not senior management. So, if your people execute the strategy, then the next logical question is: how capable are my people?

To gauge the performance of large groups of people, companies typically benchmark them using some form of measurement. Whether it be key performance indicators (KPIs), sales targets or similar, or ranking systems using a bell curve or complex 6-9 box matrixes, all methods are used to rank potential and performance.

The most common ranking system is using a bell curve to manage performance (Figure 1, page 30). If you are not familiar with this concept, this is how it works: Every person in the entire organisation is ranked based on standardised grades of performance. The result is that the top 20% are classified as talented and high potential and the bottom 10% as below average for performance management.

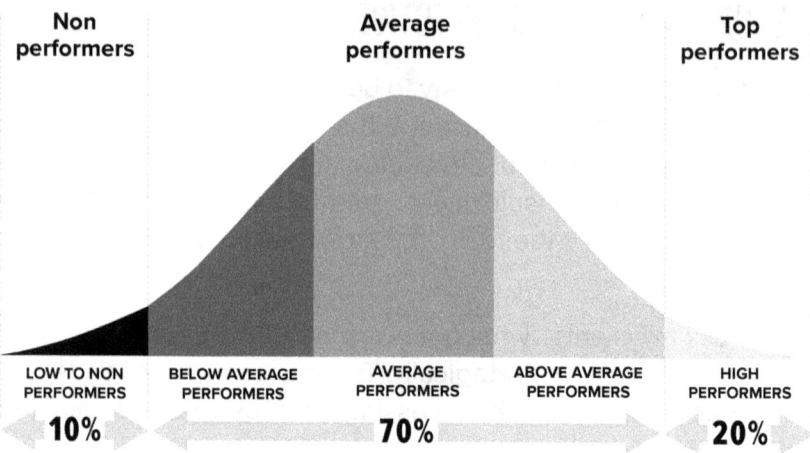

Figure 1. The Performance Management Curve

Sounds great in theory as it gives management a clear view of everyone's performance. But wait for it.

3. PERFORMANCE MANAGEMENT DOES NOT WORK

Let me explain why. Performance management systems, in various forms, have been employed for nearly two millennia. Some historians suspect it was being managed as early as 221 AD, when Wei Dynasty emperors rated their family members' performance. By the early 1960s, more than 60% of American organisations had a performance appraisal system. In most organisations today, the executive team (the CEO and their direct reports) have extra-ordinarily little time to focus on people's development and capabilities. As a result, performance management rankings are perceived as useful because it enables them to focus on the outliers – the stars and the underperformers.

The problem with this approach is that it leaves most of your people, 70%, stuck in the average performers zone. Remember, people are the key to executing your strategy. However, under the traditional performance management approach, the bulk of the workforce is provided with little development opportunities, feedback, or guidance to improve their performance.

Worst still, those caught in the 70% are sent the signal that they are not in the high performer category. You inadvertently create a new group of people who feel inadequate and fear underperforming and as such, only do what is necessary to stay out of the bottom 10%. Over time, this can be demotivating for most of your workforce.

The idea of the disengaged middle is backed by staff engagement results – a measure of how happy staff are to be working for a specific company. A score above 80% shows that staff are willing to go above and beyond what is required to achieve their company's goals, for example, happy to work longer hours or take on more work. A low score, below 20%, show they are disengaged, and below 10% means they are actively working against the company's goals, for example, complaining or avoiding work. Research by Aon Hewitt shows that the engagement rate globally has consistently hovered in the 58-65% since 2011 (Aon Hewitt, 2018). The average engagement scores mean most leaders are working with the staff that are apathetic to the company's goals.

> Imagine you are planning a road trip across the state. You have decided where you want to head, how long to stay, how many fuel stops are required, whom to bring along and what to pack. You then spend half your annual salary on a new car for the trip. The big day arrives, and you hop behind the wheel and set off. Now and then you glance at the GPS to make sure you are heading in the right direction. However, you do not pay attention to any other instruments in the car. Halfway through the trip, you feel the car is losing power, and you do not know why. The vehicle eventually stops, and you look at the instruments to realise the engine light has been on the whole time.

This result occurs across many businesses today.

Due to time and cost restrictions, the leadership teams and human resources management focus their efforts on the 30% (top 20% and bottom 10%) and leave 70% of the organisation to their own devices. Remember, a strategy is executed through all your people, not just the top 20%. Therefore, you need to stop relying on a system that leaves most of the people without any guidance and support.

This leadership vacuum is then filled by the management ranks who are left to use their best endeavours (if they are engaged) to deal with this apathetic approach (for the less engaged). The result is pockets of greatness and sub-optimal performance across different teams in your business.

You might have experienced this first-hand when working with different teams. In some teams, you can feel the energy like electricity pulsing through the air; they are focused and hungry for success. Walk down the hall and you might feel your energy drained by a team who is misaligned with each other and the company's goals. It makes you wonder how two teams within the same business can experience such differences in their outlook on work.

These variations in performance leaves you with an organisation of people – your highest costs of doing business – running suboptimally. It is like trying to drive in a Formula 1 race with a run-down sedan. When the majority of your staff feel dejected and undervalued, you can participate in the race, but have no chance of winning – without change.

CHAPTER 3

A NEW WAY FORWARD

> **"WHAT WOULD IT MEAN FOR YOUR BUSINESS IF YOU COULD HARNESS THE 70% IN THE MIDDLE AND IMPROVE THEIR PERFORMANCE EVEN SLIGHTLY?"**

By focusing on the majority, you can start to harness the power of your people to begin executing your strategy and drive results. It is time to take a different approach and unlock why, across any organisation, some teams perform well above the average, and many groups perform well below.

As my father used to say, 'When the wind blows hard, you have two choices: build a windbreak and pray it holds or build a windmill and harness its energy.' The fact that you are reading this tells me that you want to harness the wind rather than hide from it. However, you may be unsure how to harness it. I do not blame you in today's world, where new content is written every minute. It is so hard to determine what is a fad and what has a foundation.

I grew tired of seeing poor managers rise to senior roles, riding a wave of buzzwords and corporate jargon, while seeing great leaders sitting in the wings because they refused to play the corporate games. I set about trying to uncover what drives team performance and how to replicate it. Through my research, I found there were 20 different factors, ranging from having a clear sense of purpose and diverse skillset to shared leadership and clear work procedures. I put these twenty factors into a survey (Figure 2, below).

Characteristics of a High-Performance Team Survey

Please read the listed characteristics below and select the ones you believe are necessary for a high-performance team. Have you been part of or observed a high-performance team at work? If so, which of the following characteristics did this team possess?

- [ ] **Shared vision:** The team were aligned around a single view of the future/success

- [ ] **Aligned goals:** The team KPIs were clear and aligned to our vision

- [ ] **Clear purpose:** It was clear why the team were together

- [ ] **Trust:** There was a sense of trust among all the team members

- [ ] **Continuous learning:** The team was open to learning new ways and ideas

- [ ] **Open communication:** Positive and constructive feedback and ideas were openly shared

- [ ] **Productive external relationships:** The team ensured that relationships with other teams were maintained

- [ ] **Diverse Skillset:** The team had a range of skills and experiences

- ☐ **Diversity of thought:** The team could build on ideas and thoughts
- ☐ **Clear working procedures:** It was clear how things got done
- ☐ **Clear roles and responsibilities:** Everyone knew what needed to be done and by whom
- ☐ **Flexible:** The team was open to changing direction or approach when required
- ☐ **Each individual contributes:** Everyone lifted his or her weight
- ☐ **Natural agreement:** There was a consensus across the team
- ☐ **Empowerment:** The team had the authority to do what was required to achieve the goals
- ☐ **Respect:** Everyone felt respected
- ☐ **Accountability:** There was a clear sense of ownership from everyone involved
- ☐ **Shared leadership:** The leadership of the team was fluid and changed depending on who was best suited for the task at hand

Figure 2. Characteristics of a High-Performance Team

After leaders had selected which characteristics they believed would be present in a high-performance team, and then which characteristics were present in the high-performance teams they had worked with, I then asked them to rate the characteristics that were present in the high-performance teams they had led. You might like to try this now.

A leader can take a mediocre performing team and turn it around. A manager can inherit a great team and make it plummet. The common factor is the environment the leader creates around them.

To date over, 500 high-performance leaders from CEOs through to leaders of top-performing teams have completed the survey. I expected the answers to vary by organisation, team and industry. They did not. I went further and conducted in-depth interviews with leaders from some great Australian brands, as well as quiet achievers from start-up and small businesses. Their stories provide you with a look behind the curtain for how leadership plays out.

> **"It is not always rainbows and butterflies. It is dirt that gets thrown on us that helps us grow."**

The output of the research was the High-Performance Team Model (HPTM) (Figure 3, page 37). The HPTM outlines seven traits that are required to create an environment where high performance is achievable. By fostering these traits in your business, you create an environment whereby high performance can thrive and un-leash the potential of all your staff.

Wondering if you are a high performance leader? The High Performance Leader Self-Assessment (Figure 4, page 38) can be used to gauge where you and your team are right now and to see where improvements can be made. Be honest. This will give you clarity on what needs to be addressed in order to create a high-performance team. There is an online version of this survey on my website at bareinc.com.au.

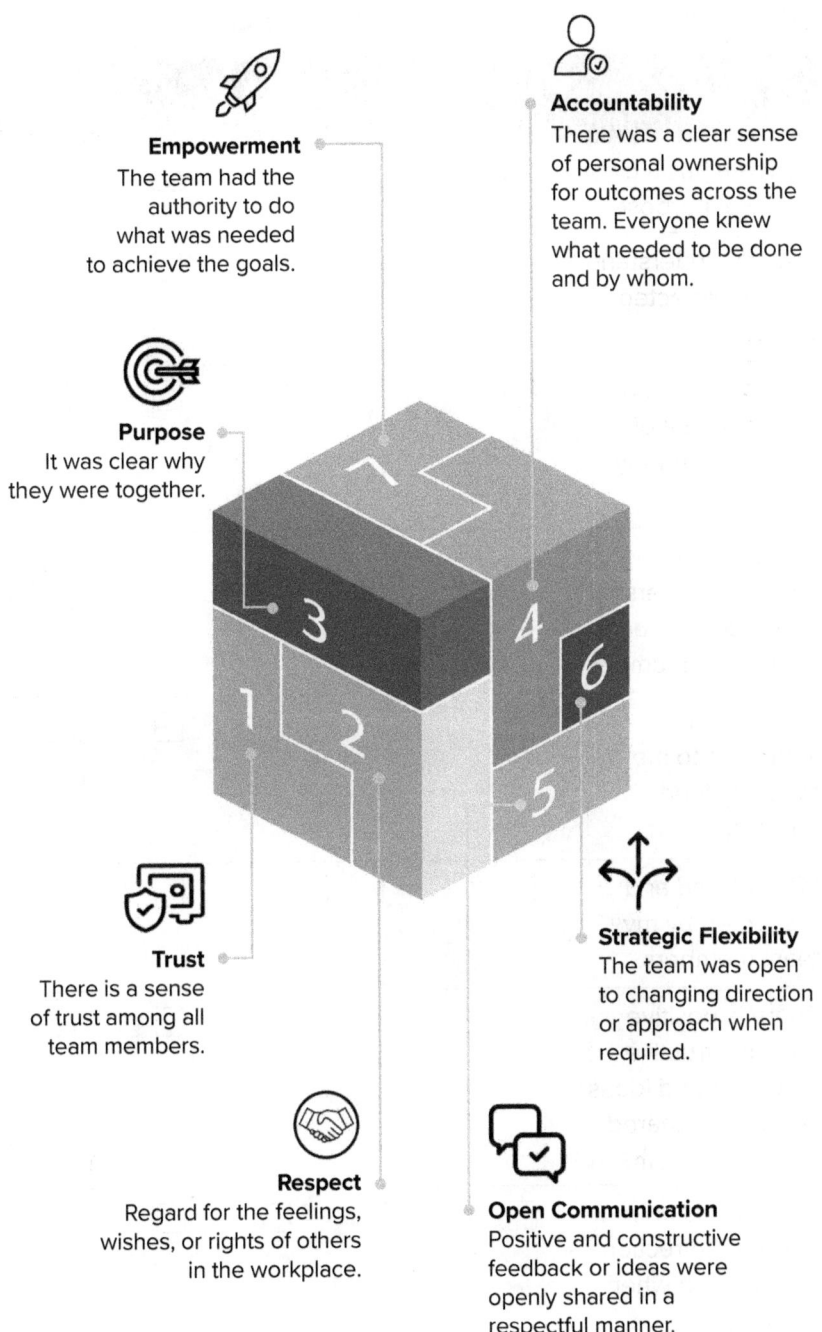

Figure 3. High-Performance Team Model (HPTM)

High-Performance Leader Self-Assessment

	Strongly disagree	Disagree	Un-decided	Agree	Strongly agree
My team has a clear sense of purpose.	☐	☐	☐	☐	☐
I clearly understand what is expected of me.	☐	☐	☐	☐	☐
It is essential that I feel a sense of ownership for my work.	☐	☐	☐	☐	☐
There is a strong sense of ownership for outcomes for each team member.	☐	☐	☐	☐	☐
At work, it is important to me to feel valued and respected.	☐	☐	☐	☐	☐
I feel valued and respected by my team members.	☐	☐	☐	☐	☐
There is positive and constructive feedback and ideas are openly shared across the team.	☐	☐	☐	☐	☐
The team is open to changing direction or approach when required.	☐	☐	☐	☐	☐

There is a sense of trust among all team members.	☐	☐	☐	☐	☐
The team has the authority to do what is required to achieve the goals.	☐	☐	☐	☐	☐

Figure 4. Leader Self-Assessment survey

It is at this point where you may be starting to identify some of your barriers. Don't despair. This book is here to support you to overcome these barriers.

In Part II, the seven traits introduced in the High-Performance Team Model (HPTM) (Figure 3, page 37) will be unpacked and explored. You will be provided with examples of how businesses have created change through knowledge and application of each trait. Practical ways to implement change in your business and within your teams will support you towards achieving a high-performance team.

You do not need to read it end-to-end, even though I would love you to do that. I know we are all busy so if a specific trait is something that you know you need to focus on to improve performance, then go straight to it and learn how to apply it. It is that simple.

> **"CHANGE IS NOT A THREAT, IT'S AN OPPORTUNITY. SURVIVAL IS NOT THE GOAL, TRANSFORMATIVE SUCCESS IS."**
> — SETH GODIN

PART II
THE HIGH-PERFORMANCE TEAM MODEL

THE SEVEN TRAITS

In Part I, you were introduced to the three barriers that prevent most leaders from creating a high-performance team. These were:

1. You lead a group of people, not a team.
2. Your strategy is ineffective.
3. Performance management does not work.

As you read Part I, you may have realised that you are challenged by one or all three of these barriers. The High-Performance Team Model (HPTM) (Figure 3, page 37) outlines the seven traits essential for creating a high-performance team environment.

Part II is structured in the order of the traits that you need to develop and master before you can move onto the next one. Each chapter follows the same structure: an overview of the trait, supporting research and a real-world case study so you can see how leaders applied it. At the end of each chapter, there is a list of practical steps you can take to replicate that trait in your business. I want you to view this as a blueprint or a handbook to drive performance.

SUMMARY OF THE SEVEN TRAITS

Trait 1: Trust

Trait 2: Respect

Trait 3: Purpose

Trait 4: Accountability

Trait 5: Open Communication

Trait 6: Strategic Flexibility

Trait 7: Empowerment

Hopefully, you have also taken the time to complete the High-Performance Leader Self-Assessment (Figure 4, page 38) either in the last chapter or on the website (bareinc.com.au). This self-assessment should have highlighted for you the key areas of focus to improve your team's performance.

Part II is specifically designed to allow you to approach change in different ways to maximise your return on effort. Determine which approach suits you.

- Approach 1 is to understand each trait and develop a practical action plan (page 179), which you can implement into your team and business.
- Approach 2 is to leverage the self-assessment and focus on the areas identified as requiring the most significant improvement. If you choose this approach, then you can go straight to the relevant trait, absorb the knowledge and develop your action plan (page 179).

Whichever approach you take, please remember: this book is to be used as a practical guide to high performance. It is not something to be read once and left on the shelf.

CHAPTER 4

TRAIT 1 – TRUST

I headed to my regular one-on-one meeting with my boss, the general manager of marketing. I was feeling quietly confident as my team was performing, and I was leading key initiatives.

On the way to his office, my phone buzzed. It was his executive assistant who advised me of a change in venue; we were meeting in a different room on another floor. I thought that was strange.

I entered the room to see the head of human resources sitting next to my boss. Taken aback by her presence, my mind recalled previous unannounced encounters with human resource managers. It usually meant something had gone wrong or something was about to go south very quickly. I calmed my nerves and asked my boss why human resources were in our one-on-one meeting. 'There is nothing to worry about', he said. 'It's just a formality, trust me.'

Trust me. The words hung in the air like a harbinger of doom.

He went on. 'You have been doing a great job, and I have no complaints about how things are progressing.' My heart rate slowed further, and I started to think that maybe I was getting a promotion.

'In fact, because of how well things are going, I have decided it is time to make some changes across the department,' he continued.

My heart started pumping faster, and I felt the promotion was within my grasp.

'Effectively immediately, we will be restructuring the entire marketing department and your role, along with a few others, will no longer exist. You are welcome to apply for any other position that you like. But there is no guarantee.'

No longer exist. No guarantee. I was furious.

Without an inch of emotion in her voice, the human resources manager then added, 'If you want to cry, you can. The other people we have already told cried a lot.'

The ripple effect from the announcements was immediate. Everyone, even those whose roles were not affected, did not feel safe or secure anymore. The overall process of defining roles, interviewing, and hiring and firing people took another four months. During this time, everyone across the department felt unsafe about their future. Some people chose not to stick around and instead found roles with other organisations. Some people were let go while others, like me, were able to secure one of the new senior positions.

The new structure was eventually in place, but the goodwill and trust were gone. Over the following two years under that general manager, the trust was never fully restored.

TRUST COMES FIRST; PERFORMANCE FOLLOWS.

As a leader, you are often busy juggling the responsibility of everything. It is easy to forget the long-term ramifications of your actions. Your actions – not words – build trust.

Trust is like a joint bank account held between you and your team. Every day, your actions and the teams' actions go towards building more trust. These actions, in turns, fill up the bank account slowly. However, like a bank robbery, if you do something that fundamentally betrays that trust, you can see the bank account emptied. You can start depositing money back into the account; however, there is no guarantee that it will reach the levels you had previously.

Trust is the foundation of top-performing teams. Ask any leader, and they will tell you that trust is essential to performance. If I asked your team how much trust they have in you, what do you think they would say?

Trust is a firm belief in the reliability, truth, or ability of someone or something. Trust is vital because it is the basis around which all human relationships revolve. Without trust, there can be no relationship. In the context of work teams, trust is one of the critical requirements in creating a high-performance team. Trust involves respect for a person, their abilities and their suitability for a role.

Trust in the workplace plays out across many levels. There is trust in yourself and your abilities, trust between you and your direct reports or broader team, the trust you have with stakeholders across the organisation, and finally, the trust your business has built up with its customers.

Let's focus on the trust that you can develop between yourself and your team. As a leader, trust must flow both ways.

In its 2016 global CEO survey, Price Waterhouse Coopers reported that 55% of CEOs think that a lack of trust is a threat to their organisation's growth. It is the elephant in the room that no one wants to address. Instead, people blame a weak economy, low wage growth and other factors outside of their control for poor business performance.

So, if many leaders feel trust is an issue, why aren't they doing anything to fix it?

The main reason for lack of action on developing trust I came across in my research was that leaders are 1) not sure where to start, and 2) operating on the belief that people trust them because they are in charge.

Contrary to popular belief, cultivating a high-trust culture is not a 'soft' skill — it is a hard necessity.

The Great Place to Work® Institute research shows that "trust between managers and employees is the primary defining characteristic of the very best workplaces." These companies beat "the average annualised returns of the S&P 500 by a factor of three." (Nusca, 2018)

If you are a leader trying to improve your bottom line, creating trust between yourself and your team can lead to triple the returns. That is an impressive rate of return on something which does not cost you money to implement.

TRUST IN THE WORKPLACE IS A SHORTCUT TO ACTION

If the team believes that each member is capable and reliable, then they are more likely to focus their energies on action rather than debating or politicking. However, a critical barrier to action is people's level of trust in themselves. At some level, as humans, we have fears and doubts about our abilities. This doubt is natural and you, as the leader, might have low levels of trust in your skills. A key to building trust with your team begins by learning to trust your capabilities. Trusting your abilities does not mean that you run head-first into making decisions. Instead, you trust that you will make decisions based on the information available at the time. If that decision proves to be incorrect, then you trust in your ability to own that decision, learn from it and take corrective action.

Your ability to build trust has a profound effect on business results because trust affects two measurable outcomes: productivity and cost. When trust goes down (in a relationship, a team, an organisation, or with a partner or customer), speed goes down and cost goes up.

CASE STUDY
LACK OF TRUST IMPACTS BUSINESS GROWTH

Two years ago, I took on a new client. She had been successfully running a jointly-owned business with her business partner for over ten years. She came to me because she was keen to take her business to the next level. My first red flag that something was wrong was that she was attending the coaching program alone, without her business partner. I asked her why, and she said her business partner does not believe that this 'stuff' works.

During our initial discussion, it became apparent that even though she and her business partner had divided their responsibilities across the business, her business partner was continually questioning and reviewing her side of the company. By putting her energy into second-guessing, it caused a slowdown in their ability to bring new services to market.

Over the next few months of working together, we identified the root cause of mistrust: her business partner's lack of confidence that she could run the business end-to-end if the other partner, my client, left. This fear manifested in her being hypervigilant of her business partner and resulted in controlling behaviour.

Once this was understood, we focused our efforts on creating new behaviours and processes to help establish trust across both sides of the partnership. These included new documentation, status reporting and timelines to get new ideas to market. Since implementing these ideas, the business has grown significantly, and the relationship between the two partners is better than ever.

The inverse is equally true: when trust goes up, the cost goes down, and speed goes up. I recently had another client in a similar industry, allied health, and again, one partner was not convinced of the value of coaching. However, their business partnership was different; he trusted his partner and came along with an open mind.

They, too, were stuck for ideas on how to take their business to the next level. Our initial session focused on setting long-term goals for the company and generating new ideas that would help them achieve these goals. Each week, the partners went away, divided up the plans and got to work implementing them. They would then reconvene with me the following week to talk through what worked, their barriers and what they would do differently to improve the results.

By taking an approach of divide and conquer, the partners were able to test a range of new ideas in the market at a much faster pace than their competitors. As a result, within three months, they had identified a handful of new service offerings that they could ramp up and quickly generate a profit.

TRUST IS EARNED

While you may consider building trust a soft skill, the benefits of achieving a high-trust environment can have a significant impact on your bottom line.

> *Six years ago, I was working on a high-profile project with the potential to deliver multimillion-dollar profits for the company. The pressure was on to deliver this project on time and on budget.*
>
> *We had a reputable, outsourced IT provider to develop the solution and a capable internal team who had been working on it for about a year. I went into the leadership role thinking it would be a manageable and sizeable piece of work that would be good for my career.*
>
> *About a month into the role of sponsoring this project, I received feedback from a source outside of the project that not everything was going as well as it seemed. She was worried that, given her junior position in the organisation, she could not come and tell me this formally for fear of reprisal. We worked in a low-trust environment, and there was a clear chain of command.*

This mistrust meant some people did not feel safe to speak up.

I found myself between a rock and a hard place. I had a reputable IT provider and a member of my team telling me everything was on track. Conversely, I had someone that I had built trust with over my time in the business telling me to dig deeper.

How would you handle this situation if you were in my position?

> **"WHEN YOU FIND YOURSELF CAUGHT BETWEEN A ROCK AND A HARD PLACE, PICK ONE AND BREAK IT."**

I had two options: the rock – let things play their course and find out later if the project was off track. This option put the already tight timeframes and millions of dollars of revenue at risk. The other option: the hard place – go against the advice of my team and fast-track an external review process to determine if corrective action was required or not. Either way, I would be sending a clear signal to someone that I did not trust them.

I chose the hard place. I sat down with my direct report, the project manager, and the IT solution provider to understand the status of the project. I did not want to blindside anyone with my doubts. To establish trust, I declared my intent. I told them I had concerns about how the project was progressing and, given how important it was to the company, we needed to ensure it was successful.

It felt like the oxygen sucked out of the room. The IT provider gave a sideways glance to my direct report, who gave them a confused look back. It felt like I had interrupted an awkward conversation, and no one knew what to say next.

Given the low trust and hierarchical nature of the organisation, I should not have been surprised that people did not want to speak up. The silence hung in the air like a cloud of thick smog, making it hard to breathe. People nervously shifted on their seats or stared blankly at their note pads. No one was making eye contact with me for fear of being asked a direct question.

Declaring my intent and trying to build trust had backfired. I took a step back and asked my direct report about how she felt the project was progressing. She said she was confident in the project and her abilities. I asked the same question of the IT provider, who gave the same response. To convey their confidence, they talked through detailed plans and ideas they had for the project. While listening to their speeches, I could not shake the feeling that they were trying to hide the devil in the detail. I tried a different tactic.

I asked both the IT provider and my project manager how confident they were that the project would be delivered on time and that the solution would work as required. This time there was no silence. The IT provider looked frustrated and revealed that my direct report had instructed them to focus on getting the project done on time. Time was the priority as their performance bonus was contingent on delivering the project by a specified date. So, I asked both of them what the likelihood of the solution working as required from day 1. The response: 2% chance. 'But we will deliver on time,' they said with a smile.

I felt the rage building up. I knew this was not going to help the situation. I immediately collected this information into a single report and took it to my boss. I explained to him the enormity of the problem. He said that my instincts had been proven right. We then mapped out a plan going forward.

My first task was to bring in a team of operators who I could trust and had worked with on other significant initiatives. Once the new team were in place, I let the project manager go; I knew we could never have a relationship based on trust after such a grievous breach.

Through hard work, extra time and more money, the project was delivered six months behind schedule. However, it was successful and exceeded the revenue targets that were forecast. It also saved the business a multimillion-dollar bill *that would have been required to clean up the mess if the original project had gone ahead as scheduled.*

The biggest lesson for me was never to put complete trust based purely on someone's word. If there are doubts, raise them and follow your instincts. That was not the first or the last time I had misplaced my trust in people. Still, I can say that tackling issues upfront, and with respect and honesty, goes a long way to building trust – both in you as a leader and in yourself for your people.

Trust forms the foundation for all other high-performance team behaviours to be built upon. High levels of trust have been linked to high performance and hence, higher returns. However, to receive trust from your team, you must first give it.

THE BOTTOM LINE: YOUR ACTIONS – NOT WORDS – BUILD TRUST

Like I mentioned before, trust is like a joint bank account. Every action and word as a leader acts like a deposit that makes it grow or deplete. Conversely, misrepresentation by either yourself or your team cannot replenish the account once emptied.

Every day your actions and the team's actions can go towards building more trust. These actions, in turn, fill up the bank account slowly. However, like a bank robbery, if you do something that fundamentally betrays that trust, you can see the bank account emptied. You can start depositing money back into the account; however, there is no guarantee that it will reach the levels you had previously.

Trust is the solid foundation from which all other behaviours are developed. High levels of trust are the foundation that ensures the organisation thrives in easy and challenging times.

PRACTICAL ACTIVITY
CREATING A HIGH-TRUST ENVIRONMENT

As a leader, you build trust with your team through your actions, not just your words. Certain behaviours and characteristics you exhibit can help instil trust in you as their leader.

Remember, trust is essential to high performance. Below is a range of behaviours you could adopt to help create a more trusting environment.

BEHAVIOUR 1: BE VULNERABLE

In a business setting, being vulnerable means being open to potential criticism and questioning. It also means you are willing to experiment with something new and accept that mistakes may happen. When you show vulnerability, it allows team members to feel more comfortable being open and honest with their concerns, questions, errors and roadblocks. This ultimately provides for a more reliable team performance.

Vulnerability is not about oversharing or talking about mistakes to gain sympathy. These actions are unlikely to establish trust, and, in fact, may even undermine it. A common issue I see with clients is that they put too much pressure on themselves to know all the answers. It is impossible to know everything.

When I was new in a role with a technology company, I explained to my team that I did not understand a term, so I googled it. A member of the group laughed. When I asked her why she laughed, she said, 'You are so different from our previous manager. He would never admit when he did not know something, let alone say he googled it.' By showing this vulnerability early, it made everyone else in the team more comfortable. It helped build trust with my team.

BEHAVIOUR 2: TAKE CARE OF PEOPLE'S WELL-BEING

Another simple way to build trust is to show you care about your team's well-being. A leader I worked for, Nick, called it, 'management by walking around'. Every day in his diary, he blocked out 30 minutes to walk the floor and chat with different people in his team. Considering his team consisted of over 150 people, that was not an easy task. When he would come back to the same person again, he would mention something that they had talked about previously to show that he was listening. Whether it was wedding plans, their kids' school or how the football went on the weekend. Over time, he was able to build a relationship with each person in the team. This led to an environment where his team were comfortable to come to him with their ideas and challenges.

BEHAVIOUR 3: GIVE CREDIT

Give credit where credit is due. Before I got my first direct report, I had the opportunity to work with another junior staff member on a project. We both worked hard on the project, but it was something that she was deeply passionate about and delivering it would help her career. When the time came to present it to senior management, I told her that they did not need two people talking them through it and that she was the best person to do it. Everyone was pleased with the outcomes we had delivered, and she received praise. After the meeting, she came to me and said that if it were not for me, we would not have delivered that result. Knowing where, to whom and how to place credit will build trusting relationships, as well as delivering higher results.

BEHAVIOUR 4: KEEP YOUR PROMISES

Nothing erodes trust quicker than a broken promise, especially if it is one of many broken promises. As such, be selective with your commitments and do not make promises that you know you cannot keep. The best leaders I have worked with always follow through on what they say. They are also transparent when making promises around the degree of success and likely risks.

BEHAVIOUR 5: BE TRANSPARENT

Be transparent while also respecting confidentiality. I have a client who reports to the CEO of her organisation. Most people in the business refer to the CEO as 'loose lips' because he is always talking about matters that should otherwise be kept confidential. During one meeting, the CEO had all but one of his direct reports in the room. He mentioned to the group that he was going to fire the other direct report based on performance issues. He then explained that he had not had the opportunity to speak to him about it yet, so he asked everyone to keep that to themselves.

Unfortunately, a week passed before the person on the receiving end of the firing received the news. By this stage, most of his peers and others in the organisation knew what was happening. Being transparent in the right situations can go a long way toward building trust. However, being too open with information you are told in confidence can erode people's trust in you.

As a leader, you need to be depositing into the joint bank account every day through your actions and words. At the same time, you need your employees to feel that they can also make deposits through their actions and words.

I know this can be a struggle when your days are long, busy and filled with lots of interactions with a range of people. Trust is the bedrock from which you will build a high-performance team and business. It would be best if you took the lead in developing this environment.

✎ **Which new behaviour will you try over the next 30 days? How will you apply it?**

_____
_____
_____
_____
_____
_____

✎ **New ideas, insights or actions to create trust across your team and business.**

_____
_____
_____
_____
_____
_____
_____
_____
_____
_____

Chapter 5

TRAIT 2 – RESPECT

She was new to the business and Arthur was keen to ensure his new colleague got off to the right start. He decided on a nearby coffee shop as the venue for their first meeting. He was keen to understand what her vision was for her new role.

The meeting was not going as expected. After the initial pleasantries, she was on her phone, tapping out messages and emails. The conversation was flowing in spurts like an old car engine struggling to keep going. Now and then, she would cut him off or speak over him to provide her thoughts and then go back to tapping on her phone.

After 20 minutes of this, Arthur decided the best thing to do was to set the tone early. He asked her to put down her phone for a minute. He explained that his intention for the meeting was to get to know her better in order to develop a strong working relationship. He stated his annoyance with her phone use during the meeting and then gave an ultimatum. 'Would you prefer we do this at another time or are you able to put your phone away so we can continue?'

She placed her phone on the table and restarted the conversation. A couple of minutes later, she picked it back up and started typing. Arthur paid the bill and left the coffee shop.

Respect manifests itself in both verbal and non verbal cues and behaviours. Have you ever used your phone while simultaneously trying to have a conversation with someone? What might seem like multi-tasking to you can be viewed as disrespectful by others.

Respect is the foundation of any thriving workplace. In any successful organisation today, you will find a diverse group of people from different races, religions, backgrounds and genders. To work effectively with such a diverse group of people, every leader and member of that organisation must operate on the basis of mutual respect. Anyone at any level in the organisation can, and should, show respect for others. Ask anyone in your workplace what treatment they most want from their bosses and co-workers and you will find that high on the list is to be treated with dignity and respect at work.

In this chapter, we will outline why respect is the foundation of a thriving team and how creating it leads to increased productivity, reduced stress levels and improved staff retention.

THE POWER OF RESPECT

Respect is a powerful force. A global survey of 20,000 employees found that respect was the number one behaviour that would lead to higher employee engagement and commitment (Porath, 2014).

In my research, we defined respect as a regard for the feelings, wishes or rights of others. In the workplace, respect comes in different forms. There is the legal requirement of respect, such as preventing racial discrimination, sexism, fair recruitment policies and working conditions. On top of this, there is respect in the form of hearing and seeing differing opinions, accepting and giving constructive criticism, and distribution of the workload.

> **"IN RESPECTFUL WORKPLACES, PEOPLE SHARE IDEAS, CONSTRUCTIVELY DISAGREE WITH EACH OTHER, AND SEEK TO UNDERSTAND EACH OTHER'S PERSPECTIVES TO DELIVER THE BEST OUTCOME."**

These behaviours also transcend beyond the company's walls and flow into how the company treats its customers, suppliers and the communities in which they operate.

Conversely, environments where there are low levels of respect can witness conflict, harassment and even bullying.

I was once part of a senior leadership team where myself and one other person (out of eleven) were from a non-Anglo-Saxon background. The manager would regularly get the other manager and I confused. Each time this happened, some members of the team would laugh. By the third time this happened, I called him out and asked him to learn our names and roles. I also pointed out that he did not seem to confuse anyone else. He responded that it was hard because 'you all look the same to me'. Again, the same members of the leadership team laughed. I don't think I have to explain that I was insulted by this response and made a formal complaint to our human resources department. They advised me that they had spoken to him about it. However, his behaviour did not change, and human resources did not pursue it further. This disrespectful behaviour set the tone for others in his management team to behave similarly. These behaviours created an environment where people would yell and verbally attack each other at work. At one point, a physically attack took place.

For employees, perceptions of respect are affected by three factors: support, collaboration and caring (Walker, 2014). Support stems from how a manager supports their employee's self-worth, professional development and provision of resources. With support also comes appreciation and recognition for a job well done. Collaboration comes in many forms, and a critical one is that the leader actively seeks input from employees about decisions that impact their work. Another key area for collaboration is how well people work with each other across the team and the broader organisation. Caring can be identified as having a leader who displays to each employee that they matter to the organisation. If you have ever worked for a company or leader and had the feeling that you were just a number, you will be aware that this feeling does not bring out the best in you. Your team wants a leader who displays a genuine interest in their success, can connect them to their purpose and is mindful of their well-being.

DEBATE, DECIDE, DO: A PROCESS FOR RESPECTFUL CONFLICT

At this point, you might think that respect means there is no conflict or that everyone has to say yes to get along. Appeasing everyone is not a sign of a respectful organisation. When staff interact from a place of respect, this does not mean that they cannot disagree on an approach to a project or policy. It just means that they tackle it civilly and respect each other's needs. "Employees better equipped to manage conflict collaboratively cope more effectively with workplace challenges and change" (Mental Health Commission of Canada, Calgary and Ottawa, 2012).

I teach my clients to encourage civil conflict using the Debate, Decide, Do process (Figure 5). This approach involves firstly having a constructive discussion on the different options the team can take. Each person can provide their opinion without fear of reprisal or ridicule. Once this stage is completed, the team then decides on an approach collectively. Again, this does not mean everyone has to be unanimous. For example, during the debate, the majority of the team may decide to go with option A. Those that chose option B need to be respectful of the decision and support going forward with option A. This brings us to the final stage, which is Do.

"AN ORGANISATION'S PERFORMANCE FLOUNDERS DUE TO THE ROT OF CORRIDOR CONVERSATIONS."

Corridor conversations refers to disrespectful conversations which occur behind a person's back about decisions made or their approach to tackling the situation. The 'Do' overcomes this as everyone has committed to getting on with the job and not revisiting old arguments.

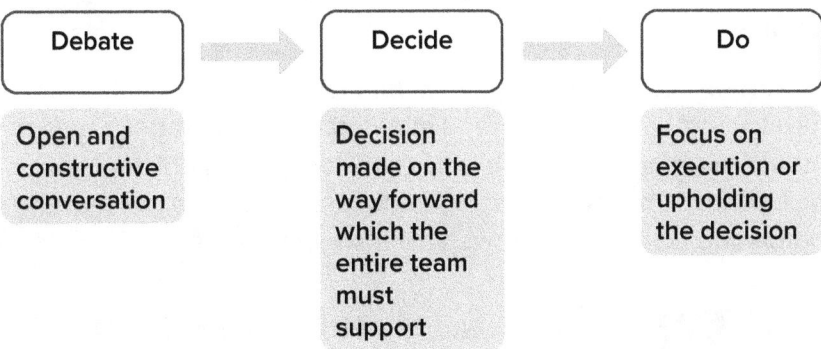

Figure 5: Debate, Decide, Do Process

The next area where respect needs to be present is the distribution of responsibilities and workload among the team.

> *My friend works in a library. She regularly opens the library, and it is a source of frustration between her and her manager. Across all of the library staff, she receives a disproportionate number of early-start shifts. When she gathered the courage to ask her manager why this was the case, her manager explained that it was to allow other staff members who have school-aged children to manage the school drop-off. Her boss' attempt to be respectful to other staff with young children inadvertently disrespected my friend by assuming, because her children were adults, she would not mind opening the library early most mornings.*

When employees receive respect from their leader and other team members, they are less stressed and more apt to apply themselves diligently to their work. The same is true when an employee knows that their superiors and business leaders respect them and their work. Employees are much less likely to perceive their workload as excessive or to submit workers' compensation claims (Comcare, 2008).

A more respectful approach from her manager would be to explain to everyone that the library needs to open early every day. By evenly distributing the early shift across all of the staff, her boss could ensure it was equitable. She could then let each staff member swap shifts with each other based on their circumstances.

In workplaces where employees feel fairly treated, incidences of hazing and harassment are eliminated. When a leader respects his or her employees, there is no room for harassment, favouritism or bullying. Instead, energy gets focused on building and strengthening cohesive relationships in the workplace.

> **"CREATING AN ENVIRONMENT WHERE PEOPLE FEEL SAFE AND RESPECTED LEADS TO INCREASE PRODUCTIVITY."**

The idea is quite simple. When people work with one another in peace and harmony, they do not have the time to focus on other shallow and petty ideas.

Furthermore, a respectful and diverse workplace is an antidote to groupthink. Groupthink occurs commonly in management teams where people come from similar demographics and socio-economic backgrounds. As a result, the combined life experiences and perspectives are similar. These similarities limit the group's ability to develop new ideas or manage risks. If you examine the boards and executive leadership teams of most businesses that failed recently despite years of prior success, it will be partly due to this. The groupthink meant they could not foresee the changes in the market or new opportunities.

Kieran and Kyle, two brothers who own and operate a successful digital advertising agency, actively rally against this idea. When recruiting, they endeavour to seek out people who they call 'different to the rest.' Kyle explained that by hiring talented people who do not fit any one mould, can lead to the generation of 'some very crazy ideas.' These ideas have meant that, as a business, they are continually innovating and delivering to customer ideas, and that these ideas are usually first to market. Everyone at the agency feels comfortable and confident to come up with new ideas because nobody is worried about what the other person is thinking. The goal is to provide the best result for the company.

> *I remember my first job when I was 18. I worked in a boutique men's clothing store ran by two brothers. Both had vastly different management styles. One brother took on the role of teacher. He would explain how to complete specific tasks and why it was essential to the company. The other brother used rudeness and threats. I distinctly remember one time he told us that if we did not hang the clothes up correctly, he "would cut off our balls." The latter approach did nothing for productivity as everyone was afraid to make a mistake, so we all worked slowly.*

The Academy of Management found that rudeness has similar impacts across both routine and creative tasks. Rudeness reduced performance on both routine tasks and creative work. Furthermore, the study found that staff who were affected by the harshness went onto to be less helpful in other situations (Erez, 2017).

CASE STUDY
MAKING RESPECT A CORE APPROACH OF DOING BUSINESS

Stuart had a great opportunity ahead of him. He was the new CEO of a newly formed retail energy company based in a remote part of Australia. Stuart had a clear strategic vision and direction he wanted to take the company. However, he had one problem. He needed to hire 60 new employees, all of whom were technically skilled, the right cultural fit and willing to work in a remote location.

Stuart knew that if he did not move quickly to build capabilities across his team, the business would soon lose customers and revenue. He was conscious of jumping in too early and recruiting people who, while technically capable, might not be the right fit for the new organisation he was trying to build. Compounding this was the remote location – a four-hour drive to the nearest town. It was going to be a tough sell to find the right people. The challenge was set and the clock was already ticking.

Stuart knew that, as the leader, he was responsible for team selection and this duty could not be delegated to human resources or outsourced to recruitment companies. His approach to recruitment was simple. He worked on the assumption that each person coming into the interview room was technically capable. Once they were in the interview room, he focused on the 'human side' – specifically, he wanted to understand what their values were and ensure that respect for oneself and others were at the core of them.

It was a lesson he had learned from his previous role. He had built up a group of champions but not a champion team. While each member of his group was talented and highly capable of delivering, the group did not operate well with each other. Going forward, he wanted to change all that.

Once he had recruited most of the team, he set about determining the core values for the new organisation. The process for creating the values was going to run in parallel to building the business strategy. Stuart knew that how they achieve their results was just as relevant as what they accomplished.

Traditionally, this task of creating the organisation's values included the CEO and their direct reports, in conjunction with the human resources team. The process usually resulted in a set of three to five values being communicated across the business. Stuart did not want the usual posters on the walls and pats on the back for the executive team. In contrast, he felt creating the values in this way alienated most employees, who often do not understand how these values translate to their daily work.

Stuart took an unconventional approach and empowered the staff to determine the company values. Given the integral role the company played in the community and with the government, it was no surprise that respect came out as one of the core values. It also helped that Stuart had purposely hired talented people he knew held respect for others as their core value.

He then took this a step further and had each team define respect in terms of the behaviours they would accept and the actions they would not. This definition was crucial because 'the standard you walk past is the standard you set'. By having each team define respect, it provided a consistent explanation of respectful and disrespectful behaviours. It also meant that discussions around these behaviours were had upfront rather than after a problem had arisen.

By defining, documenting and sharing these behaviours, it meant every team member had a clear understanding of what it meant to operate with respect. Stuart took another step forward and enshrined these behaviours into employees' bonus structures that said they could not receive their full bonus without behaving respectfully. By incorporating these behaviours into a financial outcome, Stuart was able to focus the team on creating a respectful environment as opposed to managing cases of harassment or bullying.

To support the leaders in his organisation with these changes, he rolled out training that helped them deal with situations where behavioural issues occurred. This approach also meant that when employees encountered behavioural problems, it was not a conversation about punishment. Instead, each leader received training so they could learn how to best support their team members live the company's values.

It was also reflected in the conditions of future employment with employees made aware that their employment could be terminated for breaches of the core values of the business. In instances where employees consistently did not meet the values, they were let go from the business. Letting go of people who did not meet the behavioural expectations sent a message across the organisation that respect was at the core of how they operate.

Stuart's approach ensured he created a thriving culture that focused on driving the right outcomes for customers and the business.

THE BOTTOM LINE: RESPECT IS A POWERFUL FORCE

You have learned that respect is a powerful force. It can have numerous benefits across your organisation from reducing stress and promoting innovation to increasing productivity, profits and staff retention.

As a leader, you will influence the way the people in your team feel about your organisation and the time they spend at work. At work, people need to feel comfortable to be able to express their ideas and work with dignity and respect.

PRACTICAL ACTIVITY
CREATING A RESPECTFUL ENVIRONMENT

Here is what you can do to create a respectful environment (Figure 6).

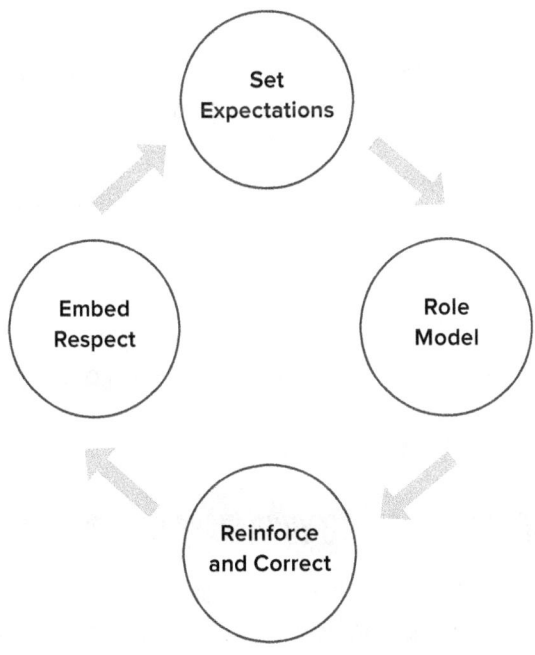

Figure 6. Four-step Cycle to Creating a Respectful Environment

STEP 1: SET CLEAR EXPECTATIONS

First, you need to set clear expectations of behaviour. Like the approach taken by Stuart, you can have the team define and provide examples of respectful and disrespectful behaviour. You can use this approach when forming a new team or working with an existing group or organisation. The exercise can also be used for existing groups to reinforce the importance of fostering respect. It could be an agenda item for each team meeting.

The goal is to develop a shared understanding of appropriate conduct at work and what these expectations mean in a practical setting.

STEP 2: BE A ROLE MODEL

The next step is to be a positive role model. If you are respectful, employees are more likely to follow. If you are abrasive and impolite, employees have an excuse for displaying the same behaviour. Be genuine in your actions and promote the kind of culture that inspires people to do their best.

STEP 3: REINFORCE POSITIVE BEHAVIOUR AND CORRECT BAD BEHAVIOURS

When a person is discourteous, unconstructive or abrasive, have a conversation with the team member to name the specific action and the impact the behaviour is having on you or the team overall. Letting the behaviour go is viewed as condoning it and lowers the standard for future behaviour.

STEP 4: EMBED RESPECT INTO YOUR WAYS OF WORKING

Focus on incorporating these behaviours into your ways of working. For example, include behavioural expectations in performance plans and give regular feedback to employees relating behaviour and expectations to performance. Some of my clients split their performance review and bonus payment into two categories: what you achieved and how you achieved. Some go further and ensure that staff cannot receive their full bonus unless the 'how you reached it' score is high.

✎ **Which new behaviour will you try over the next 30 days? How will you apply it?**

_____
_____
_____
_____
_____
_____

✎ **New ideas, insights or actions to create respect across your team and business.**

_____
_____
_____
_____
_____
_____
_____
_____
_____
_____
_____
_____

CHAPTER 6

TRAIT 3: PURPOSE

What am I doing here? Emma asked herself as she stared at yet another iteration of the advertisement. It was one part of a much bigger puzzle she was trying to develop. Emma knew she was running on empty. The long hours were starting to take a toll both mentally and physically. She was stressed, tired and on edge, but she knew she had to keep pushing.

Emma was clear on her purpose, and it was that fire that drove her to work late into the night. She was trying to get 1000 girls sponsored by International Women's Day; an ambitious goal her organisation, the Australian arm of a global charity, had set itself. She knew of the life-changing benefits child sponsorship had, especially on young girls, to break the cycle of poverty. That was what kept on driving her to make it work.

On the other side of town, in a plush conference room, Hayley was waiting for the CEO to address the room on the new direction of the business. The CEO came to the microphone and declared the purpose for their energy retail business was to beat the competition. The room was silent for a moment, and then everyone clapped and nodded their heads obediently.

'What am I doing here?' Hayley asked herself. She enjoyed her job and loved her team. She was seeking a sense of purpose for her work and beating the competition was not it. She knew then that she was going to have to create it herself so both she and her team could thrive. The problem was that she didn't know where to start.

DO YOU HAVE A SENSE OF PURPOSE DRIVING YOUR WORK?

In the two examples above, each company could argue they have a purpose. The first organisation's focus is on breaking the cycle of poverty through child sponsorship. The second organisation's purpose is to beat the competition.

The energy company's purpose, however, lacks clarity. For a company's purpose to be useful, it needs to form a rallying cry for everyone across the organisation. Merely stating 'beat the competition' does not provide any clarity around what they need to focus on.

The purpose is open to interpretation, and different leaders across the business did just that. The head of the customer service team focused on beating the competition by reducing the costs associated with servicing customers. This purpose led to significant scale reductions in customer service staff and long phone wait times. However, it meant that his area had the lowest cost to serve in the industry.

At the same time, the marketing department interpreted the purpose to mean positioning themselves as a premium provider in the marketplace. They acted by increasing the price of their services. In the short term, this led to increased profits.

Fast forward 18 months and the company was indeed beating their competition; however, it was on the wrong metric: customer churn (the number of customers leaving the business for a competitor). They were market-leading with customers fed up with the poor service and high prices.

Unperturbed, at the next gathering of the company's leaders, the CEO stated their company's purpose was mostly unchanged, their focus was to be different from their competitors.

The CEO was operating under the old paradigm of business — that business fundamentally exists to make money.

PROFIT VS PURPOSE

You may be thinking that having a purpose beyond making money is a bit wishy-washy; the feel-good stuff that does not benefit the business. Many executives view their relationship between their company and their employees as pure economics. In that, the employees are paid to do a job and they are there to do that job, preferably with the least amount of effort required by the company for maximum benefit. Most employment contracts outline this economic value exchange. The company pays a salary for a prescribed set of hours worked each week. An employment contract does not state anything about the company honouring their purpose and operating in a way that instils trust with their employees.

However, if you asked most employees why they work for an organisation, it is unlikely they would say that it is because they have a contractual agreement. Instead, they would give reasons such as the company culture, alignment of the company's purpose with their own, its leadership, or the exciting and challenging nature of the work. These are also some of the reasons employees cite for leaving an organisation.

For 50 years, companies have focused on putting shareholder's interests first. The concept of a company and a team having a purpose, beyond making a profit, is still relatively new.

Unfortunately, when you peel bare the purpose of most organisations, it is to make money for their owners. That is why most organisation have key performance indicators that use an economic measure (cost or revenue targets). These measures are easily measurable and cascade through all levels of the organisation.

> **"LITTERED THROUGHOUT HISTORY ARE EXAMPLES OF COMPANIES MAKING RECORD PROFITS AND PAYING OUT MASSIVE BONUSES TO EXECUTIVES WHILE SIMULTANEOUSLY LAYING OFF STAFF."**

This approach is not limited to large corporations either. There are numerous examples of start-up companies where founders paid themselves huge salaries while running the company into the ground. For an increasing number of companies, the pursuit of profit is no longer enough.

If you asked your team, 'What's the purpose of our organisation?', how would they answer?

It was not until the global financial crisis (GFC) that the pursuit of returns for company owners and shareholders, at the expense of others in society, started to show cracks. A study conducted by Ernest and Young and Oxford University Saïd Business School found the public conversation about purpose increased fivefold between 1995 and 2014 (EY Global, 2018).

A PURPOSE IS ESSENTIAL

Having a clear purpose is a driving force that propels teams to higher performance and helps them push through the inevitable tough times and obstacles. This said, it is interesting to note that many clients come to me because they struggle to find a sense of meaning to their work.

For my research, I defined purpose only as 'it is clear to all team members why they are together.' I used this definition because it distils it to the purest form – that feeling you get when you think about why you work for the company.

Ingrained in our psyche is the need to seek a sense of purpose from our lives. In a 1943 paper called *A Theory of Human Motivation,* Maslow presented the idea that our actions are aimed at goal attainment (Maslow, 1943). Maslow's Hierarchy of Needs (Figure 7) has often been represented in a hierarchical pyramid with five levels.

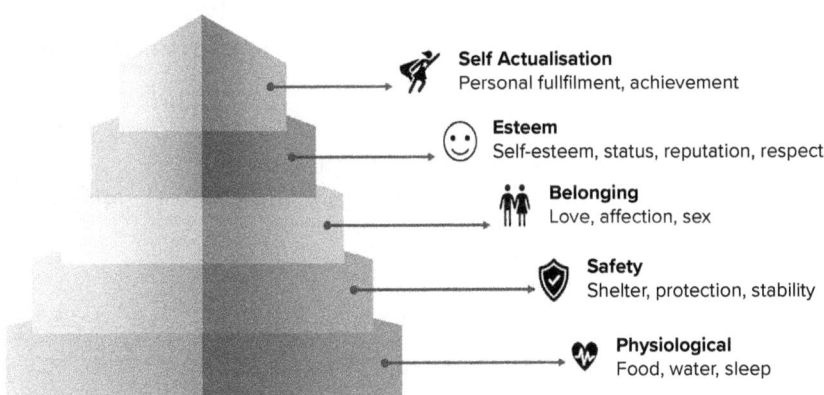

Figure 7: Maslow's Hierarchy of Needs

The three lower levels (lower-order needs) focus on physiological needs. In contrast, the top levels of the pyramid are considered growth needs. For a person to progress, they first need to meet their lower-order needs. For example, if I have no food, I will focus my efforts on ending my hunger, rather than finding my dream job.

The base level, physiological needs, includes air, food, water, sleep and other factors towards homeostasis. Once achieved, people shift their focus to the next level. Safety includes security of employment, resources, health and property.

From there, people shift their focus to belongingness, which includes love, friendship, intimacy and family. Then onto esteem comprising of confidence, self-esteem, achievement and respect. The highest level of the hierarchy is self-actualisation, which takes in morality, creativity and problem-solving.

Considering we spend nearly a third of our lives at work, it is natural that we should find a greater sense of purpose from it.

Unfortunately, some managers drive their people's performance by focusing on safety needs. The use of key performance indicators and ranking systems are a subtle way of reinforcing an employee's psychological need for safety. This is executed by assigning an employee a set of objectives that they need to meet over a 6-12-month period. These usually include some form of financial measures, sales revenue, or cost management and performance-based deliverables. The explicit message these send to the team is evident – achieve these objectives, and you will be considered safe with the organisation; do not deliver on these areas and you will not be secure.

> **"AS HUMANS, WE ARE ALWAYS SEEKING A SENSE OF PURPOSE; A MEANING TO OUR LIVES."**

However, achieving these key performance indicators does not guarantee your safety. I have worked in organisations where everyone was ranked against each other. This ranking process creates an environment where no one is ever safe, and people are encouraged to go above and beyond what is required. The issue with these environments is that they can cause ongoing stress, which ultimately results in poor performance and can lead to burnout.

Conversely, some organisations do not have key performance indicators or objectives. This lack of clarity creates much angst among employees as there is no clarity around what a safe outcome looks like in their role.

As you become more successful in your career and your needs transcend beyond making money for security reasons, you start to seek out a more profound meaning from your job or work. The same applies to those you lead. The more senior and successful you are in the organisation, the more likely you will attract more talented operators. These people, in turn, will be seeking something more substantial than a paycheque, for sacrificing a third of their lives.

PURPOSE AND PROFITS

A ten-year study across 50,000 brands found a positive relationship between a brand's ability to serve a higher purpose and financial performance. That is to mean, brands that focus on doing something more in society than simply maximising profit, performed financially better than those that focus solely on profits (Macquarie, 2017).

When most people think about purpose-driven organisations or brands, they usually think about charities or not-for-profit organisations. However, many other brands are operating under a highly purpose-driven philosophy.

> *A great example is Dove.*
> *Have you ever thought about what the purpose would be behind working for a company that makes soap and hygiene products?*
> *Dove is using its brand to help improve the self-esteem of girls worldwide. They have recognised that low self-esteem is a massive problem for females. When you visit their website, you learn how serious the problem is.*
> *Through their #speakbeautiful movement, Dove seeks to help girls gain more confidence in their beauty. On social media, women tend to express negative thoughts about their looks. The #speakbeautiful movement encourages these women to use social media to say positive things about themselves and others.*
> *Now, can Dove say this purpose directly drives a profit for their business? Probably not. But it makes their brand relatable to their target market: young women. Dove is also attracting talented employees from around the globe. They want to work for an organisation that is having an impact on the world, while also making money.*

PURPOSE DRIVES STRATEGY AND INNOVATION

A clear purpose has benefits that extend beyond merely making money. The first is providing everyone in the organisation with strategic clarity. As I said earlier, your strategy is executed by your people throughout the organisation, not just the executive team.

Having an articulated purpose makes it easier for employees at all levels to align their daily activities and decisions around that purpose. An articulated purpose keeps organisations focused on driving long-term, sustainable value, rather than short-term gains. Purpose also works as a means of setting boundaries for what an organisation will and will not do as part of its growth strategy. These boundaries become particularly crucial for organisations that operate in highly competitive industries, where everyone is looking for an edge.

Another area which benefits from purpose is innovation. As well as driving incremental improvements to products and services, purpose can inspire original ideas and creativity in an organisation. Guided by purpose, employees can be empowered to recast themselves as problem solvers and value providers.

A great example of this came from the head of products at a leading technology company focusing on job seekers. During a leadership team meeting, everyone was discussing new ideas and the conversation became heavily focused on driving short-term revenue. The founder of the company overheard this conversation and told everyone in the room that the company's purpose was to connect talented people with the right role in the right company. He urged the team to focus on developing the right solutions and the revenue will come. He cautioned that if they were to focus on delivering short-term revenue at the expense of the customers, there might not be any customers in the future.

CASE STUDY
CREATING PURPOSE ACROSS A HUMAN RESOURCES TEAM

A great example of creating and driving a sense of purpose is Damian, a Human Resources Executive for a group of national retail shopping centres.

Human resources are viewed as the department that other managers and leaders go to when they need expert support to engage their staff. When Damian took on his new role, the team he was leading had just come through a merger. It was apparent to him that despite the merger, they were two vastly different organisations and being spread across two separate office buildings further deepened the divide. After surviving the merger, the human resources team emerged with a lack of purpose, direction and energy.

With the human resources team unengaged, a broader issue arose for the business as leaders in other areas could not lean on them for support. Damian knew there were many smaller tribes – groups of people – that made up any organisation. Before he could drive wide-scale change across the organisation, he had to start with his tribe.

The first goal was to bring them together as a team, rather than a group, and have them all working towards a single goal and purpose. To do this effectively, Damian had to start building new relationships with each member of the group. First, he organised individual meetings with every team member to understand what their purpose was for coming to work. Damian was trying to uncover their underlying reason for coming to work – their WHY.

Everyone's WHY was different. Some wanted to master the skill of human resources management; others saw it as a safe profession.

Upon completing the initial phase – determining each member's purpose – Damian examined all the specific reasons why people came to work and tried to align it with the team's purpose. The current team's purpose, 'Everyone deserves to go home', was focused heavily on ensuring that everyone had a safe working environment, and people remained injury-free.

Keeping everyone safe at work was essential; however, it did not inspire the entire team. Many of the team found that this purpose focused only on a subsection of the workforce. Furthermore, the team felt they could not actively contribute to bringing this purpose to life. For example, the people who worked in payroll administration felt powerless to ensure a builder constructing a new store, was safe at work.

For Damian, it became clear that to get the team re-engaged, he needed to create a new shared purpose. Armed with the knowledge of individual purposes, he tasked his leadership team to create new purpose statements. Damian then did the unusual step of putting the team's purpose out to a vote across the team.

Based on the votes, the team selected their new purpose, which was 'Create an awesome place to work.' By co-creating an original purpose, Damian ensured there was alignment across the team.

To bring the purpose to life, he worked with each team member to determine how they would contribute and embody this in their everyday work. By connecting their purpose statements to the team's purpose, it created a sense of personal accountability. Each member of the team was willing and responsible to bring the team's purpose to life every day at work.

A common complaint the human resources team received was that the first paycheque of new staff was delayed because it took so long to get set-up in the company's payroll system. This experience was far from their purpose of making it an excellent place to work. Invigorated with their newfound purpose, the payroll department proactively reviewed their processes and made it simpler for staff. As a result, every new staff member received their first payment on time. This change ensured that staff where happy and helped reinforce that they made the right decision to join the business.

However, this process of aligning individual and team purpose was not all smooth sailing.

Some staff found that their purpose no longer aligned with the team's purpose and where the broader organisation was heading. This misalignment created a dilemma for Damian. Through a series of discussions with each person, it became apparent to both them and Damian that it would be best if they parted ways. Damian then assisted each staff member to find a new role and company which was better aligned to their purpose and could leverage their technical skills.

Through hard work and consistent effort over two years, Damian lifted the team's engagement rate to world's best practice.

THE BOTTOM LINE — A SENSE OF PURPOSE BENEFITS ALL

We are wired to find a more profound sense of purpose and fulfilment in our lives. The need for purpose applies particularly to our work, where we will most likely spend a third of our lives.

Having a clear purpose can have benefits across all areas of a business:

- Staff morale
- Strategy
- Innovation
- Profits

Companies that have a clearly defined purpose and leverage this in their everyday decision making outperform the market over the long term. Beyond financial results, companies with a clear purpose can also drive strategic clarity, transformation, innovation and improve relationships both inside and outside the organisation.

PRACTICAL ACTIVITY
CREATING A TEAM PURPOSE

STEP 1: FIND YOUR PURPOSE

As humans, we are always seeking a sense of purpose – a meaning to our lives. When you consider how much time we spend at work, it makes sense that we would want to find meaning from our work.

When my clients are feeling deeply frustrated with their work, it usually stems from a misalignment between their purpose and their company's purpose. However, if you and the company's mission are aligned, then you are connected to something broader than your everyday work. People are more likely to feel engaged in their work if they can clearly understand how their work is helping to create a better future for the organisation.

If you are not sure about your purpose, the following approach can help you. I have used this strategy with many of my clients. The concept is called Ikigai (Figure 8), a Japanese term that roughly translates to "reason for being."

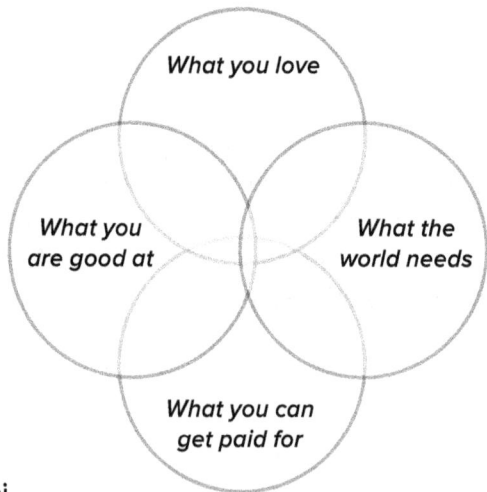

Figure 8. Ikigai

I love this approach because it provides a workable model through which to find your purpose. The model focuses on finding the balance between the spiritual and practical aspects of your life. Specifically, the balance is at the intersection of four areas: what you love, what the world needs, what you are good at, and what people will pay you to do.

If you find yourself staring at the diagram and wondering where to start, go old school with a pen and paper and ask yourself these questions:

- What would I do even if I were not paid?
- What do my family and friends say I am good at or should be doing as a job?
- If I won the lotto, what would I spend my time doing?
- What activities make my soul come to life?
- What is my perfect day?

Once you are clear on your purpose, I recommend you write it down as a single statement. That way, you can reflect on it when times get tough, or you need to make difficult decisions.

I recommend you start by doing this process yourself and develop a clear understanding of your purpose. Then, it is vital to understand if your purpose aligns with your company's purpose. You may find that your purpose aligns with some or all of the company's purpose, which is excellent. Conversely, you might discover through this process that your mission and the company's mission are not aligned.

This misalignment can cause frustration. Your choice is to live with the misalignment or to find a company that aligns with your values. It can be tough to authentically lead if you do not believe in your company's purpose.

 Take time now to populate the Ikigai to help you find your purpose, using the blank Ikigai.

My purpose
_____
_____
_____
_____

STEP 2: FIND INDIVIDUAL TEAM MEMBER'S PURPOSE

Once you have established your purpose, you need to do the Ikigai process with each member of your team. If you operate a large team, you might do this with your leadership team (direct reports) only. Doing this individually with each member of your team will reveal one of two things. Firstly, it should tell you what they are genuinely passionate about and their purpose. Secondly, you can use this information to identify if each team member's mission aligns with the company's purpose.

Where a close alignment exists, explore how their role plays a part in bringing the company's purpose to life daily. Making this connection will help people connect to something broader than their function. People are more likely to feel engaged in their work if they can clearly understand how their work is helping to create a better future for the organisation.

In instances where there is a misalignment, it does not mean that the staff member needs to move out of the organisation. Misalignment could be a trigger to alter their role dimensions, to enable them to do work they are passionate about. There may be a more suitable role for them in a different area of the business.

If you find there is no alignment, the best choice of action for both you and the staff member is to part ways; however, breaking up is never easy. You will need to do this respectfully by following the company's human resource policies and relevant laws.

It is important to remember when completing this step to treat each member as a whole person, not a specific role or collection of talents. At work, it is easy to view the person as the role; for example, Jane does payroll. Then we mistakenly assume they would want the next promotion above them.

I fell into this trap when I was working with a talented sales operations analyst. Her role focused heavily on gathering and analysing data. As part of her development plan, I assumed her next logical role would involve a broader remit and direct reports. However, six months into this role, she was unhappy, especially with leading people. By sitting down with her and going through this process, we discovered that her real passion was guiding people's health and well-being through yoga. To fulfil her love, we focused on what aspects of the role she could further develop, and then assisted her to transfer into a new career running a yoga practice.

STEP 3: CREATING A TEAM PURPOSE

Great work! At this point, you are now clear on your purpose and each member of the team is clear on their purpose. The focus now shifts to developing a team purpose. Here are the steps to creating a team purpose:

1. Each team member (or if it is a large team, break them into small groups) develops two team purpose statements. Have them write the statements on post-it notes or paper cards.
2. Each team member or group share their purpose statements with the rest of the group.
3. Group similar purpose statements together to determine common themes.
4. Vote to find the two most popular purpose statements.
5. As a group, take aspects you like from the two statements and refine them into a single purpose statement.
6. Do not settle for a statement that everyone is ok with as this will not drive team cohesion. The litmus test is when you read the statement out loud, do you feel a resounding "Yes! That is what we do"? If not, keep going until everyone, including yourself, feels it.
7. Stress test the purpose statement by using real-world examples for how you could bring this to life, either within the team or for customers or stakeholders your team interacts with frequently.
8. Seek feedback from key stakeholders or senior management to ensure they buy into the new team purpose.
9. Communicate the team purpose broadly across the organisation and frequently within the team.

New ideas, insights or actions to create purpose across your team and business

Chapter 7

TRAIT 4 – ACCOUNTABILITY

Sarah was confident and knew that controlling the processing and the people meant you controlled the result. She liked to give orders and made sure her team followed them.

The new company she joined had a vastly different culture to her previous organisation. Her sales department was responsible for selling complex technology solutions to large brands across the country. The solutions her team sold were not cheap; however, they delivered the results that customers wanted.

The sales team was driving double-digit growth for the last three years but were still a small part of the broader organisation.

Playing small was not going to cut it for Sarah. She had big ideas and even bigger ambitions. This role was her first executive role and she was keen to make her mark early.

During her first week, she ensured she met all her direct reports to get the lay of the land. Her direct reports explained they had a clear team purpose of fostering meaningful relationships with customers. They explained that much time was required to develop these relationships, which meant for some customers, the sales revenue was small. They also explained that under their approach, each salesperson had ownership of their targets and how to achieve it.

To Sarah, this approach sounded soft and fluffy. To Sarah, sales were about having a precise target and having strong management oversight to make sure the team were doing the right thing, and consequences when things went wrong.

She knew from that first week that she had a big challenge ahead of her.

During her second week in the office, she noticed that the sales team usually worked from their desks and were not on the road like her old sales team. This different approach made her uncomfortable. To reduce her discomfort, Sarah had two options: she could work with the sales team to understand why they approach sales this way, or she could change their behaviour to match her previous sales team approach.

It was clear to Sarah what needed to happen. She convened the national sales team and gave them a directive. From now on, she did not want to see them in the office. Their role was to be on the road, meeting with customers daily.

She explained that to ensure adherence to the new directive, each salesperson now had a target number of customer visits they had to make each day. The team were shocked and did not understand why she was providing a directive before she had even spent any time with them to understand their roles. Despite this, the team gave her the benefit of the doubt. From the very next day, the sales staff took their new directives on board and tried filling their calendars with client meetings.

Two months passed, Sarah was feeling more comfortable; the team were on the road a lot. However, she noticed that the team's sales were not increasing as expected.

Sarah was perplexed. This approach had worked previously, but it was not working now. She came to her logical conclusion: the team must not be conducting the sales visits properly. This reinforced her belief that if you want people to do their jobs properly, you had to control how they did it.

She issued a new directive. All staff had to input meeting minutes, ideas, and customer feedback into the customer relationship management system daily. This additional data would provide Sarah with the further insights she needed to see who was doing their jobs properly. To ensure adherence, the data input became a mandatory requirement to receive their sales commission. Anyone who was caught not inputting their data would not receive their monthly sales bonus.

The sales team were growing increasingly frustrated. They were losing more and more ownership of their role. The sales team already felt that Sarah did not trust them to service the client's how they saw fit. Now on top of this, they had to spend a couple of hours each day writing up meeting notes, leaving them with even less time to do customer visits.

By month three, Sarah received her first customer feedback. Customers were growing frustrated by her sales team, hassling them to meet and not caring about the quality of their relationship.

To ensure these complaints would not happen again, Sarah made an example of the sales agents responsible for these accounts by naming them at the monthly sales meeting. She stated clearly that they were not up to do their jobs if the customers were complaining.

By month six, staff morale had deteriorated further as a result of having lost any ownership of their role. They were punished for making mistakes and publicly praised for achieving targets. The culture in the team had changed from being highly accountable and sharing ideas to fearful.

A handful of her top performers left the company. The company practice was to conduct an exit interview, where the leader could get direct feedback from the leaving employees. The feedback is used to improve the situation for the remaining team members. Sarah did not hold these interviews. If people wanted to leave, then they were not tough enough to survive in her sales team.

By this point, the customers had also had enough of the sales approach. They felt the team had become too focused on driving short-term sales at the expense of their relationships. Customers started finding alternative businesses to meet their needs.

Sarah was growing frustrated at her team's lack of ability to generate sales. She made a drastic decision to offer their products at a high discount, sometimes up to 50% off the usual price.

A new directive went out: all salespeople were to offer customers a discounted rate to buy their products over the next three months. Her sales team questioned the logic of providing substantial discounts to all customers, especially those who were already spending with them. She disregarded their feedback and told them to start making the discounted offers to customers.

The heavy discounting worked, creating an uplift in sales. Sarah felt she had made the right decision, and she was not concerned that substantial discounts would dramatically decrease the department's profit. She needed to make her mark. The discounted sales offers lasted three months.

By now, most of the sales team felt like they had lost all ownership. They were told what and how to sell and punished for not achieving their targets. The sense of shared accountability and trust across the team were gone.

After a year in the role, all the high-performing salespeople had left the organisation. Sarah struggled to recruit new salespeople, as word had spread about her highly controlling and punitive management style. The profitability of the department was continuing to fall, and they were losing more customers.

At this time, Sarah was let go from the organisation, having been responsible for reversing the strong sales growth and dramatically deteriorating profit in the department.

HOW MINDSET IMPACTS ACCOUNTABILITY

A significant contributor to Sarah's downfall was her inability to let go of control. Her insecurity that she would not be needed if the team succeeded without her micromanagement created a death spiral. It is this fear that ultimately keeps these managers stuck at a certain level in their career and stifles the performance and professional development of their team.

The original intention of flattening organisation's structures was to provide staff with less management bureaucracy and more autonomy to get things done. However, what I witness happening time and time again are managers and their teams falling into two groups: those with a fixed mindset around their roles, like Sarah, and leaders and teams with a growth mindset.

Managers and teams with a fixed mindset focus on doing things the way they have always been done and avoid change. This fixed mindset is commonly brought to life with sayings such as, 'sorry that isn't my job' or 'our department does not handle that. You need to find someone else to help you.' These managers and their teams are usually not doing this out of spite for the organisation. Instead, they are using their fixed mindsets to provide a form of psychological safety. They reason that by not going outside of their defined boundaries, they cannot get punished by their manager or the organisation for doing their job. This approach can cause frustration and inefficiency across the organisation and within the team.

Conversely, some leaders and teams relish the idea of taking on new challenges and are not restricted by what was in their position description. These leaders and teams actively work to fill the gaps to achieve an outcome. They have a growth mindset, and they believe, through dedication and hard work, they can develop new abilities.

Across my spectrum of clients from small businesses to large corporations, I have seen people both overextending and shunning their responsibilities. Having a defined role is vital in helping you and your team understand what needs to be achieved.

However, creating a sense of accountability that transcends the role definition and links back to a purpose is essential.

In the previous chapter, we discussed the importance of having an articulated purpose – both for yourself, the team and the broader organisation. Once you have a purpose in place across all levels, you can focus on aligning individual roles to bring that purpose to life.

In this chapter, we focus on the importance of defining roles and ensuring people feel they are accountable to deliver to those roles. That is, knowing how each team member contributes to the higher purpose of the team.

Given this is an important topic, we will explore the concept of role clarity. Once that is understood, we will shift our focus to the interrelated idea of accountability.

High-performance teams do not try to do everything. Instead, they decide what is important, who will do it and then deliver it to a high standard.

> **"IF THE FUNCTIONS IN YOUR TEAM DO NOT SEEM CLEAR TO YOU, THEN THEY ARE PROBABLY UNCLEAR TO OTHERS."**

In my research, I defined the role of clarity as everyone in the team knowing what needed to be done and by whom. A study found "role clarity moderated the prospective relationship between role efficacy and role performance effectiveness in the predicted direction for offensive role functions. Individuals who reported higher role clarity also reported higher role efficacy and performed better than those with lower role clarity" (Bray, 2002). What this means in plain English is that people who were clear on what their role was within a team were able to be more effective in that role than those whose role was unclear.

Think about your team: how many of them are clear about their role?

Now, I want you to consider whether this role clarity is aligned with your company's purpose?

> **"WHEN THERE IS ALIGNMENT BETWEEN ROLE CLARITY AND THE COMPANY'S PURPOSE, IT MAKES IT EASIER FOR INDIVIDUAL CONTRIBUTORS TO COLLABORATE."**

Collaboration improves when the roles of individual team members are clearly defined and well understood. High performers enjoy positions where their role boundaries are enough to allow them to perform most of their tasks autonomously. Without role clarity, team members waste time and energy negotiating what is in and out of their role. To those with a fixed mindset, they will work to protect turf, rather than focusing on achieving the company's goals. You may have seen this play out either within your team or in other departments. People argue over trivial matters and then miss out on opportunities. By spending the time to define roles and responsibilities, a great deal of that energy becomes accessible for other purposes.

David, who is a captain in a metropolitan fire brigade, recalled a scene to me they recently encountered.

The fire had already gone through the ground floor of an office building and was quickly taking over the second floor. The flames were bursting through the upper storey windows, and the larger licks of the fire looked like they wanted to jump across to the neighbouring business – a panel beating shop. Given that there were many chemicals and paints stored at the panel beating shop, everyone knew that a top priority was to stop the fire before it could reach the adjoining shop.

David told me that when the trucks roll up to a scene, no one on board knows what to expect. However, they have confidence that each team member knows their role and this role is matched with relevant training and experience. Before their boots hit the ground, each team member knows who will take command on-site, who will be entering the property and who will be operating the equipment from the truck. They have such a high focus on role clarity because they know it saves lives – not just the lives of the people they are there to help but also their own and that of their colleagues.

> **"AN ORGANISATION THAT SPENDS TIME PROVIDING ROLE CLARITY IS FIREFIGHTING."**

David explained to me that it is not like the movies where the truck rolls up, everyone jumps out and they all run into the fire, making plans on the fly. Instead, he said that there is always someone outside of the fire in a command role directing everyone. That person may give an order to break through a wall in the house. While the firefighter is responsible for executing the order, they must put the safety of themselves and their team first, based on their first-hand knowledge of being in the fire.

By being clear on their roles and responsibilities, they can apply this to any situation and adapt their approach based on who has the most knowledge and capabilities for any given situation.

CASE STUDY
CREATING ACCOUNTABILITY ACROSS THE MARKETING DEPARTMENT

Fiona had recently joined a large insurance company as the head of marketing. During her initial conversations with the CEO and colleagues, she soon uncovered that the marketing department had a reputation of being slow to market and driven by a 'decision by committee' approach.

Within her first four weeks there, she noticed this too. Everyone felt the need to be involved in every decision. The modus operandi was: if unsure, get more people in the room to talk about it.

Her team were fatigued from having to take carriage of all of these projects but never being able to make decisions themselves. They felt like they were running fast on a hamster wheel with more work coming and nothing new getting to market.

While the inclusive nature of the culture was something she did not want to lose, she felt there was a better way of getting decisions made. She needed to strike a balance between the business' need to provide input with the speed of products to market.

The first step in resolving this challenge was to understand the roles of each team member and what their responsibilities were in making different decisions. What she found was that while there were position descriptions in place, they were inconsistent. Each person interpreted their role differently, and there was not a clear outline of what each team member was responsible for doing or deciding. It was clear that her team lacked role clarity.

As a result, she set about developing a consistent position description by job type for every member of her team. She also added a new section into each position description titled Decision-Making Authority. The decision-making authority section outlined what decisions the team member could make and when to escalate decisions to their manager.

Once she had provided role clarity, she focused on creating role clarity for the other departments that interacted with her marketing team. However, it is essential to note that she did not try to define each department's role holistically. She focused on where she would get the most effective outcomes by scaling the approach she had used with her team across departments. This defined their responsibilities for interactions with the marketing department and introduced them to the concept of decision-making authority when dealing with marketing activities.

To give an example of how this new role clarity was applied, the pricing team were now only responsible for checking that marketing was showing the correct pricing information on their materials. Previously, the pricing team were able to provide feedback on a broad range of areas, from initial strategy and tactics through to colours and imagery used in specific marketing pieces.

By doing this across her marketing team and the broader areas that impacted her team, Fiona was able to streamline their workload and increase their speed to market. Specifically, she brought down the number of people required to sign a piece of marketing collateral from 23 to 7 people. Furthermore, she ordered the approval process. This meant that the relevant people approved the technical information, such as legal and pricing information before it went to other areas. These changes ensured that people seeing the material later in the approval process were not spending time reading legal terms and conditions or cross-checking pricing. Fiona then gave each person a 48-hour window to provide sign off. These changes meant Fiona was able to reduce the total number of days for approval from 6 weeks to 10 days.

The changes Fiona put in place also reduced the level of stress and frustration across the teams as everyone involved understood their part in the process. Her team felt more empowered in their roles and used their extra time and energy to focus on improving relationships with key stakeholders and developing new marketing strategies.

IS THE LEADER ULTIMATELY ACCOUNTABLE FOR EVERYTHING?

As a leader, you might have heard the term 'the buck stops with you'. At work, being accountable for everything can be difficult when many issues occur outside of your sphere of control. As a result, leaders can waste copious amounts of energy, and have an increased level of anxiety, over concerns they cannot control. This situation, in turn, takes them away from focusing on what is within their control and actioning the ideas that will have the most significant impact on the business.

It is for this reason that the first half of this chapter focused on role clarity. By setting clear boundaries around what you and your team are required to achieve, it provides everyone with defined limits in which to concentrate their efforts. Furthermore, it becomes much easier to hold people to account when it is evident what they are responsible for achieving.

In the modern workplace, a lack of accountability has numerous drawbacks for businesses. The Workplace Accountability Study (2014) found that organisations with low levels of accountability are often plagued with "misalignment around key priorities and desired results." It stated that there was a consistent decline in staff engagement levels across the organisation and that low levels of engagement lead to low levels of trust and cross-functional collaboration across the organisation. The ineffective partnerships meant that the execution of critical initiatives was often inefficient. The combination of these factors can then lead to "high turnover due to confused expectations and poor management practices" (Partners In Leadership). In a nutshell, it creates a terrible place for anyone to work.

For my research, I defined accountability only as 'There was a clear sense of personal ownership for outcomes across the team.' I used the terms ownership and accountability interchangeably because, in my mind, they are the same thing.

Do you agree?

LOCUS OF CONTROL

In my coaching practice, when clients come to me with their challenges and goals, they generally fall into one of two camps. Some say, 'I know I need to improve and I am willing to put in the work to get there' and those who say, 'I do not know why this is happening and I wish something would improve.'

Notice the difference? The first type of client is putting accountability on themselves to change their situation. In contrast, the latter is placing their hopes on something in their external environment miraculously changing.

Psychologists and coaches call this the locus of control (Figure 9). The locus of control is an individual's belief system regarding the causes of his or her experiences and the factors a person attributes success or failure.

Divided into two categories, the locus of control is either internal or external. If a person has an internal locus of control, that person attributes success to his or her efforts and abilities. A person who expects to succeed will be more motivated and more likely to learn. The internal locus of control is remarkably like the previous concept of a growth mindset.

A person with an external locus of control attributes his or her success to luck or fate and will be less likely to try to learn (Phares, 1974). The external locus of control is remarkably like people with a fixed mindset. People with an external locus of control are also more likely to experience anxiety as they believe they are not in control of their lives.

It is too simplistic to say that an external locus of control is terrible and an internal locus is good. However, research shows that people with a more internal locus of control seem to be better off; for example, they tend to be more achievement oriented and attain high paying jobs. Taken to an extreme, people with a high locus of control can over inflate their role and fall into the trap of thinking everything that went wrong was their fault.

External	Internal
Locus of	Locus of
Control	Control

Outcomes outside your control – determined by "fate" and independent of your hard work or decisions

Outcomes within your control – determined by your hard work or decisions

Figure 9. Locus of Control

You might be wondering how this applies to the idea of accountability. When you examine the make-up of most high-performance teams, you will find that they have an internal locus of control.

Take a moment and think about your team and where their locus of control might fit? I want you to think about them on a scale of 1 to 10.

A team that sits between 1 and 5 will have an external locus of control. These team members will likely believe that what happens to them is the result of luck, fate, or is determined by people in authority. They may tend to give up when things do not 'go their way,' because they do not feel that they have the power to change it.

To overcome this, pay attention to their language and self-talk. When you hear the team say things like 'I have no choice' or 'There's nothing I can do,' step back and remind them that they can always make choices. Help them to set goals and note their progress. You'll find that their self-confidence quickly builds.

You may find it useful to develop decision-making and problem-solving skills across the team. These tools can enable them to take greater ownership of situations, rather than blaming circumstances or forces 'beyond their control' when things go wrong.

Teams with a score of 6 to 10 have a moderate to high internal locus of control. They will likely feel that they are in full control of the events in their life. They are self-motivated and focused on achieving the goals they have set. You will most likely hear these people say, 'I can fix that issue' or 'do not worry, I know what needs to get done.'

A downside to a high internal locus of control is the team member may have such a powerful self-belief that they find it difficult to take direction, or they walk over others to achieve their goals. A robust internal drive may lead them to believe that they can control everything. If their plans do not work out, they may feel responsible for their failure – even when events were genuinely beyond their control. This internal drive can lead to frustration, anxiety and, in extreme cases, stress or depression.

> **"FEW PEOPLE HAVE A WHOLLY INTERNAL OR EXTERNAL LOCUS OF CONTROL – MOST OF US FALL SOMEWHERE BETWEEN THE TWO ENDS OF THE SPECTRUM."**

Your locus of control may vary in different situations (for example, at work and home), and it may change over time. People often tend towards a more internal locus of control as they grow older, and their ability to influence the events in their lives increases.

During my corporate career, I came across managers and departments that I would describe as 'all care, no responsibility'. This phrase means that while I may be worried about something or want something to change, if I am not responsible for it, I will not do it. An example I witnessed every day in the office was when the printer ran out of paper. Some people will leave it for the next person to fix because it is not their job. These are the same people who usually get the most frustrated when they need to print and there is no paper.

As a reaction to a lack of accountability, most organisations revert to using responsibility as a punitive measure. A multi-year study of 40,000 participants, found "accountability is something that happens to you when things go wrong, rather than something you do to yourself to ensure results" (Nurmesniemi, 2015).

As a leader, I implore you not to use accountability as a punishment for when things have gone wrong. Instead, leverage people's internal locus of control to create a rewarding environment for people who show high accountability. The rewards are especially important when people take managed risks, and things go wrong. Use this as a learning opportunity to determine what went wrong and how they can handle it differently in the future.

According to a survey conducted by AMA Enterprise, a division of the American Management Association®, business leaders recognise a lack of accountability on the part of employees. The managers surveyed felt that nearly one-third of their employees avoided taking responsibility (American Management Association, 2016).

Now, whether almost a third of the staff are unaccountable is hard to measure, however, the fact that their manager thinks they are will create mistrust between the manager and their staff. To learn more about this, see Chapter 4 Trust.

THE BUSINESS CASE FOR ACCOUNTABILITY

My research found that high levels of accountability were critical to the performance of a successful team. A study from the United States Office of Personnel Management found that using accountability as a reward improved performance, morale and innovation (United States Office Of Personnel Management).

A great example of this was Toby, the CEO of realestateview. Toby is known as a straight shooter who always delivers on what he promises. After leaving another technology firm to lead realestateview, he was keen to instil this same sense of ownership across the new business.

Toby explained that 'accountability means people can count on one another to keep performance commitments and communication agreements.' He had a simple ask for every employee across the business: be clear on what you are committing to achieving. He iterated, 'if it looks like you might not realise a goal, communicate clearly and early so we can help.' His approach focused on encouraging people to step up and take ownership without the fear of reprisal if things went wrong. This approach started to foster a new environment in the business where there was increased synergy – a safe climate for experimentation and change – and improved solutions because people felt supported and trusted. All these positive processes create higher employee morale and satisfaction.

CASE STUDY
CREATING ACCOUNTABILITY IN RETAIL BANKING

The personal lending team had gathered around a small meeting room to hear the latest business update. Things were not going well for them. Their business unit was losing money every day, creating an unfavourable position with shareholders and nervous vibes around the office.

It came as a surprised when their general manager visited to informed them that a new boss had been appointed. Emma was not what they expected; she was young and had a reputation as a rising star in the bank's consumer finance division. Hence, the surprise that someone would willingly take on the role of heading up their division.

Emma knew she had many challenges ahead of her. Earmarked for senior management roles, the competition to secure these senior positions would be hard. That is why she volunteered to take on a failing division; she needed to prove that she could turn things around, to set her apart from the pack.

The bank's mission was to be the best in every field that they competed. The underlying message to this purpose was: if you are not going to be in the number one spot, then get out of the market so we can redeploy our resources elsewhere.

The personal lending division was far from 'the best'. It was losing money every day, suffering from high processing times and low staff morale. Emma's manager was running out of patience and had given her twelve months to turn things around. On top of this, Emma had never run a personal lending team before so she was about to ride on a steep learning curve.

Emma's first instinct was to run a large-scale process improvement project across the entire division. She had successfully implemented this in her previous role and saw some great results. However, when she discovered the former manager had already tried this approach and failed, her hopes faded. The option put forward was to develop a new digital system that would be the magic bullet to all the problems in the division. So, Emma set about discussing this previous project with her management team. She quickly learned that all the ideas for improvement had come directly from the last head of the division, with no consultation from his direct reports. That had left each staff member feeling disenchanted and powerless to help. This view had then slowly spread across their teams. The entire division was viewing themselves as victims of circumstance with no control over their destiny.

Emma knew that the only way to turn this perception around was to put the team in the driver's seat. They needed to take accountability. To start this process, Emma asked each of her direct reports to come with a list of their most significant challenges. Each brought a list of challenges that they wanted her to solve. Instead, she got each of them to pick the smallest problem on the list and determine a way to solve it. She purposely had them chose a minor challenge because she wanted each team member to have a taste of success. This approach is called the snowball effect: you start small and, as the wins start coming, people's confidence grows, which in turn gives them more confidence to take on more significant challenges.

Emma did this each week until the only challenges left were the most significant. At this point, she asked her direct reports to share their most significant problem with their teams and their peers in the division. She also asked them to solicit ideas to solve them. This approach created a sense of shared accountability, and soon people were sharing ideas across teams and working overtime together to solve problems. By aligning people to a broader purpose, everyone was keen to fill any potential gaps and help each other increase their overall performance.

The teams came up with solutions to problems that were specific to their team. For example, a solution put forward by the credit assessment team to increase the quality of data from the sales team was for the credit assessment team to run monthly training sessions around the importance of proper data collection and its use. This training fostered a sense of accountability in the sales team as they realised the better the quality of data collected, the faster the loan would be processed. Quick loan processing meant the sales team would receive their commissions faster. It created a win-win situation for all involved.

To further drive the sense of shared accountability, Emma set up a simple whiteboard where she listed all the significant challenges. Every time one of the challenges was overcome, the team would get together and celebrate. The act of striking a line through a difficulty further reinforced that everyone was in control, and together they could achieve more.

As a result of this approach, Emma was able to bring the average processing time down from 14 days to 2 days. Furthermore, the level of fraud dropped as the data collection improved. Staff morale increased and over time the division was buzzing with people sharing ideas and having fun at work.

More importantly, Emma was able to turn around the bleed in cash and the business started to grow. After two years, it gained so much momentum that she was promoted out of the role and into a more significant senior management role in their wealth division. Which, at the time, was in desperate need of a turnaround...

THE BOTTOM LINE – ROLE CLARITY ENSURES ACCOUNTABILITY

Organisations plagued with low responsibility often have low staff engagement levels. Low engagement levels weaken cross-functional collaboration. As a result, the execution of critical initiatives becomes ineffective. The combination of these factors then leads to poor management practices and high levels of staff turnover.

Conversely, my research found that high levels of accountability were critical to the performance of successful teams. Leaders of these teams benefit from improved performance, higher levels of employee participation, and increased commitment to work, staff morale and levels of innovation and creativity.

By aligning an individual's role to the team's purpose and the company's purpose, you help people become accountable. They feel they belong to something larger than just their function.

To operate at a high level, you need to remove the ambiguity and be clear about people's roles and responsibilities. Role clarity ensures that everyone knows what they need to do. Ideally, they are each individually playing to their strengths. When everyone knows what to do, collaboration improves, and an increase in collaboration means that less falls through the cracks.

After implementing the activities outlined in this chapter, you would have built two critical building blocks of a high-performance team: a clear sense of purpose and accountability. In the next section, we shift our focus to the third area, creating a trusting and respectful team environment through open communication.

PRACTICAL ACTIVITY
CREATING ACCOUNTABILITY IN YOUR TEAM

The following three activities will help you create a high level of role ownership across your team.

ACTIVITY 1: ALIGNING ROLES TO PURPOSE

The first step is to align the team's role with the purpose you created in Chapter 6.

Examine each role in the team and determine the top 2-3 activities/deliverables you want each position to be conducting. Write each one on a separate post-it note or spreadsheet.

Next, gather your team and have each member write down the 2-3 most important tasks they currently perform.

You will now have two sets of post-it notes, which outline what you want the team to be delivering and what they are currently focusing on. Next, as a group, identify the gaps between what needs to be happening and what is presently happening. Then brainstorm potential reasons or causes for these gaps. For example, lack of role clarity can lead to not enough resources in the team to handle the workload, which could mean there are missing capabilities in the team.

Once you have identified the critical causes for these gaps, you can then brainstorm possible solutions to address each deficiency. Use this information to either refine or create new position descriptions for each team member. Also, ensure to align each position description with the team's purpose and the company's purpose.

ACTIVITY 2: CREATING CLEAR POSITION DESCRIPTIONS

One of the best ways to provide your team members with clarity and accountability is to write a great position description that is well understood and regularly reviewed.

The development of a useful position description is an essential organisational tool. Ultimately, time taken to communicate internal roles allows your team to understand the position they hold in the overarching company strategy. By feeling a part of this strategy, employees are motivated to grow and succeed with it. Employee role descriptions set expectations for staff and easily allow management to recognise achievements as well as under-performance.

A position description should provide the team member with an understanding of their role by providing information that clarifies and describes the job, its functions, the work environment and reporting relationships.

Consider the following when creating a position description.

The position description should:

- reflect the needs of the work area and describe the position, not the incumbent
- use language and content that is correct, up-to-date and reflects the level of responsibility and outcomes expected
- avoid gender-specific language
- be in a concise and summarised format
- limit the use of jargon and acronyms
- include potential exposures and requirements for the role
- list only the inherent requirements of the job.

Once completed, you can effectively set a position title. The position or job title needs to reflect the role and responsibilities of the individual accurately. Ultimately, a position title needs to articulate where an employee stands in the overall company hierarchy.

After the position title comes a position statement. This statement is a further iteration of the team member's title. It summarises the purpose of the position and how this employee fits in with the rest of the working environment and business goals.

Alongside responsibilities, I recommended that my clients always include a section regarding role expectations. Role expectations differ to role responsibilities in that they articulate tangible tasks the role requires.

ACTIVITY 3: DEFINING DECISION-MAKING AUTHORITIES

With role clarity in place, you need to focus on defining who is responsible for making various decisions across the organisation or within departments.

My preferred approach is to create a RACI chart (also known as a RACI matrix or diagram). RACI is an acronym for Responsible, Accountable, Consulted and Informed. Put simply, it is a tool that identifies roles and responsibilities against tasks within a project or department.

The RACI chart maps tasks and deliverables against roles on your project, and decision making and responsibilities are allocated to each position using the above terms. So, let us look at what each of these terms mean.

Responsible: This is the person doing the task. They are responsible for getting the work done or making the decision. It can sometimes be more than one person, but the number of people involved should be minimal.

Accountable: This is the person who owns the task. This person or role is responsible for the overall completion of the job or deliverable. Ideally, this should be one person rather than a group to avoid confusion in terms of who owns the task. In my experience, this person is usually the head of the area or project team.

Consulted: This is a person or people who provide valuable information to the group or can act as subject matter experts.

Informed: This is a person or group who need to be updated on the progress. They are not asked for feedback nor are they to provide review or approval. A typical example of this might include interest stakeholders or other departments who have an interest in knowing how the initiative is progressing.

RACI is particularly useful for large departments — multi-disciplinary cross-functional teams with multiple people. I do not recommend using this approach for small, nimble teams.

Responsible
Does the work to complete the task.
Accountable
Delegates the work. Is the last one to review the task or deliverable before it is deemed complete.
Consulted
Provides input based on either how it will impact their work or area of expertise.
Informed
Needs to be kept in the loop, but does not require details to any considerable extent.

Example: RACI for a Car Trip

Jane is organising a car trip with her friends: Jack, Charlie and Emma. Jane is accountable for ensuring that the whole trip goes smoothly. However, she does not want to do all the work herself, so she has assigned the following roles to others.

- Charlie is responsible for fuelling up the car and selecting the music.
- Jack will be driving and is responsible for supplying the snacks for everyone.
- Emma will be the navigator.

Here is the same information laid out in the RACI matrix.

Table 2. Example of a RACI matrix

Activity	Jane	Jack	Charlie	Emma
Put fuel in car	A	C	R	I
Driving	A	R	C	I
Navigation	A	I	I	R
Music	A	C	R	I
Snacks	A	R	I	C

The RACI matrix provides a visual representation of how each person needs to interact with others to complete the task correctly. You can see from the matrix (Table 2) that Charlie is responsible for getting the fuel. He needs to consult with Jack, who is driving the car, to make sure it is the right type of fuel. Emma is overseeing navigation. She informs people of the route but does not need their input.

CREATING YOUR OWN RACI MATRIX

STEP 1 : IDENTIFY ROLES

Think about who is involved. Create a table listing the roles at the top.

STEP 2: IDENTIFY TASKS OR DELIVERABLES

Review the project and break it down into precise tasks and deliverables. Write these in the left-hand column of your chart. Where possible, try to keep these as key deliverables; do not become too granular.

STEP 3: ASSIGN THE RACI TO EACH ROLE AND TASK

Work through each task and think about the different roles and who should be responsible. Every job or deliverable should have a Responsible and an Accountable, at least. Make sure there is only one role or name assigned to Accountable. This is important. Think carefully who should be Consulted while the task is ongoing, and who should be Informed once the job is complete.

STEP 4: AGREE ON THIS WITH YOUR TEAM

Agreement with your team is essential. Align any assumptions you have made with your team – do not do this solo. If you have not gone through roles with people, have a quick chat through how you have set up the RACI and make sure everyone is happy with their roles and responsibilities on the project.

STEP 5: AGREE ON THIS WITH CORE STAKEHOLDERS

Set up a call or meeting to agree on the RACI with the core stakeholders.

ACTIVITY 4: THE 50% RULE

The last activity focuses more on shifts to people's mindset when it comes to accountability. Remember when we talked about people's locus of control? People can switch between internal ('this is up to me to fix') and external ('everything that has happened is outside of my control').

A method I found useful in creating a consistent approach to accountability was the 50% rule. The 50% rule states that when there is a problem or you are setting a goal, and there is more than one party involved, then each party is responsible for half of the outcome, 50%.

I like this approach as it encourages everyone involved to take some ownership of the result. It also prevents people who have a high internal locus of control from overextending and taking on the problem or solution solely. Conversely, it forces people with an external locus of control to think about what is within their control.

A typical example I came across in my career was the sales results, or more specifically, not achieving a sales target. The missed goal triggered the blame game – the sales team blaming the marketing team for not doing enough and the marketing team blaming the sales team for not selling the product correctly. This circular argument leads nowhere, and everyone is left frustrated. By applying the 50% rule, I would encourage my marketing team to examine what they could do differently next time to improve the result. Inevitably they would find things that were in their control, for example, which customers were targeted with the offer or how the proposal was communicated to specific customers. Similarly, the sales department would come up with initiatives to improve the results within their control, such as consistent sales training around new product launches.

When applying this rule, individuals or teams must come up with ideas that are in their control. By focusing on what is in their control, it ensures that each person or group takes ownership and then implement the relevant actions.

New ideas, insights or actions to create accountability across your team and business

CHAPTER 8

TRAIT 5 – OPEN COMMUNICATION

In a leadership role, you are bombarded by communication continuously. There is an endless stream of emails, phone calls, meetings, chats or instant messages. The irony is, despite the overwhelming amount of communication, the leaders I work with feel that they are not always receiving the right information. They also worry that what they are trying to communicate is not reaching and engaging their team. At some point, it can all begin to feel like noise, and it becomes difficult to cut through.

> **"DO YOU EVER FEEL OVERWHELMED BY THE AMOUNT OF INFORMATION YOU RECEIVE?"**

I also hear the flipside from staff in the organisations I work with. They can feel management is not being open with them about how the business is performing. As a result, staff are living in a constant heightened state of alertness, waiting for significant changes to occur without warning. As a result, they are not putting all their energy and efforts into performing at their peak, as they are distracted with what might go wrong.

Open communication occurs when all parties can express ideas to one another, such as in a conversation or debate. On the other hand, in a high-performance team setting, we describe this as positive and constructive feedback or as ideas that are openly shared.

> **"AS A LEADER, HOW YOU COMMUNICATE GOES WELL BEYOND YOUR WORDS."**

People consider your body language and even the energy you permeate to understand the underlying message. You might have worked for someone that, as soon as they enter the office, you know what mood they are in even before they open their mouth. You may have experienced it when someone tells you something, but your gut instinct feels that something is not right. Your brain is reading the non-verbal cues and sending you a warning.

Open communication can thrive once you understand that everyone absorbs information differently. Some people prefer to talk openly about issues and ideas. Others prefer to read and digest information and then come back to you later with their ideas well formulated. As the leader, it is your role to understand the communication preferences of your team and key stakeholders and adjust your style accordingly.

At this point, you might be questioning why it matters?

My research found that high-performance teams tend to communicate openly, promptly and with the intent that the feedback and ideas improve the performance of the organisation. Other studies have shown similar results, and there is a definite link between open communication and financial performance. While achieving open communication might sound complicated, it does not need to be.

Dominic is the CEO of an energy company that has been growing consistently by 20% year-on-year. As Australia is one of the most competitive retail energy markets in the world, this is an impressive result.

He attributes part of this success to the company's core value: 'We are one team.' From open-plan offices and no closed-door meetings, Dominic makes sure the value of one team is brought to life every day.

At the core of Dominic's approach to open communication is the belief that team members want to understand two aspects of the business. Firstly, the objectives the company is trying to achieve, and secondly, how the company is performing against those objectives. His view is that no one, including himself, should be surprised by the results, therefore – good or bad – the news is communicated.

Every Monday, Dominic does a six-minute podcast on how the business is performing, industry updates and other news or ideas he feels is relevant for staff to know. He ensures the podcast is authentic by writing a couple of bullet points and then talking freely.

Dominic knows that people absorb information differently, and he is comfortable with the fact that not everyone will listen to the podcast at the end of the day. As such, he ensures there are multiple forums where people can provide feedback. The different communication platforms include a short daily meeting called a stand-up, where everyone discusses the priorities for the day ahead. There are also more formal financial and budget review meetings through casual monthly catch-ups over food and drinks.

By providing numerous forums and platforms for staff to provide feedback, it ensures Dominic, as the CEO, is never surprised. It also means that bad news does not blindside the team and that when hard decisions are needed, the team already has context. By creating a trusting environment where there are no surprises, the staff feel safe to not only get their job done but to do it well.

LOOK FOR THE SIGNS

How do you know if you are in an environment where people do not communicate openly? The signs that you and your team are not openly communicating include decisions being made unilaterally without context or consultation. When asked why there needed to be a quick decision, a common reason given is lack of time to explain the details to everyone. From a leader's viewpoint, I can understand this: time-crunched, a quick decision is seen as the right decision. Unfortunately, this approach usually results in the team wasting time resisting the decision rather than supporting it. This resistance might not be visible to the leader. It might show up as corridor conversations, passive-aggressive comments or, in worst cases, people disengaging from their work.

> *Phil wanted to restructure the team to ensure they would continue performing at a high level. He knew what was required based on his knowledge of the organisation. As a result, he announced a raft of changes to roles across his department without consultation.*
>
> *One of these team members, Simon, not only missed out on the promotion he was expecting, he ended up reporting to one of his colleagues. For Simon, this was a demotion but he did not feel he could verbalise his issues with Phil. Phil noticed over the coming weeks that Simon was getting more annoyed each time Phil requested things from him. He also noticed that Simon was coming into work later than usual and leaving earlier. Instead of addressing the issue head-on, Phil left the situation expecting the emotions to die down and everyone to get on with the job.*
>
> *Three months after the announcement, Simon's performance had degraded to the point where he was now at risk of being performance managed out of the organisation. Phil wondered how his once strong performer had got to this point, and Simon felt angry and unsupported by Phil.*
>
> *In this situation, Phil had achieved his objective of putting the new structure in place. However, he did not realise his goal of improving the team's performance.*

Time can be the enemy of quality, but it does not have to be that way. I tell my clients that it is better to stop and take a little medicine as soon as you start feeling sick, rather than ignoring it to get worse and then requiring more medicine later. In Phil's example, the lack of open communication does not only impact the relationship he has with Simon, it had broader implications across his team.

A lack of open communication erodes trust. You are taking money out of the joint bank account that you have with your team. Take too much out and staff tend to disengage and hold back their thoughts for fear of retribution. They may also begin to feel that management no longer has their best interests in mind, and become wary of offering anything over and above the minimum contribution. Good ideas that stem from the individuals who know an organisation most intimately – the employees – are the lifeblood of any business. To lose the steady flow of insights and innovations unique to your business is a sure path to static, or worse, arrested growth.

This situation creates a downward spiral as the management then begins to see the team's performance degrading. Management starts to believe that the team are not performing to the best of their abilities and hence, do not have the best interests of the company at heart.

While it is not appropriate to always consult on every decision, you need to consult on and communicate decisions that have far-reaching impacts. It is helpful for team members to understand the underlying rationale for every decision that impacts them.

SAVE THE SURPRISES FOR A BIRTHDAY PARTY

During university, I worked in a customer service role in a call centre. It was an easy role and the management were always supportive. During one shift, the management team were asked to gather for a briefing from the general manager.

Everyone huddled around the small speakerphone. A few people questioned why the general manager was not present in person.

The general manager advised the management team that it had been decided that our department no longer fit into the company's strategic direction. As such, effective immediately, they would be closing the entire department.

The mood in the room quickly turned from jovial to sombre. Most people were in shock, trying to process what they had just heard. The general manager went on to ask us to pass on to all staff to please pack up their belongings immediately, adding that anyone who refused would be escorted out by security.

He told us he wanted to get the message out this evening before everyone went away for Christmas break. It was Christmas Eve, and I still remember the raw emotions, tears and anger from some people in the room. Some staff had been with the organisation for over a decade. There was utter disbelief that management would communicate this over the phone on Christmas Eve. The staff were expected to go home and tell their families that they had lost their job the night before Christmas.

Unfortunately, it was not the last time in my career that I would witness such poor communication. Effective open communication stems from a place of respect and trust. Correctly executed, open communication further reinforces mutual respect and trust.

Balancing trust and open communication is a delicate task. To get this balance right, various factors need to be considered, such as the nature of the topic, the type of project, team members and their dynamics and the work environment. I do not want you to get to this point and assume that all communication needs to be free. Indeed, there is such a thing as too much information. A common pitfall with open communication is breaching confidentiality.

> **"AS A LEADER, YOU NEED TO DETERMINE WHICH TOPICS ARE SENSITIVE AND WHICH ISSUES REQUIRE A CONFIDENTIAL CONVERSATION."**

Breaching confidentiality is a common pitfall for leaders and their teams. You may have found yourself on the receiving end of a conversation that starts with 'keep this between us. I will be making the following changes to people or teams in the business.' Next thing you know, someone else is coming to you asking if you have heard the news about the changes to the team structure.

Being told something in confidence, only to find out other people have already heard it or different versions of it, does not build trust. An easy way to overcome this is to state that this information is confidential, and it should not leave the room.

The second pitfall of open communication is that you elicit too much feedback from people and decisions cannot be made. For example, Jesse works in an organisation where it is common for up to twelve managers to be in a meeting to discuss a potential project or issue. Despite not being impacted, each manager has an opportunity to give feedback. This approach then snowballs when each leader brings their team into the conversation to provide feedback. The result – decisions are not made until everyone agrees. This process significantly slows down the decision-making process and means that the feedback provided is not always valuable or necessary.

ACTIVELY SEEK FEEDBACK

Another common barrier with surfacing feedback is dependent on the superiority hierarchy – people are fearful of communicating with people above them in the chain of command. If trust and respect have not been established, open communication may be hindered by fear and a lack of confidence to speak up. To avoid being viewed as incompetent, people may sweep issues under the rug instead of raising them with their manager.

The issue of losing face can be particularly crucial across different cultures. The loss of face was an issue Henry, the CEO of an Australasian technology company, faced with his international team. The Australian team were comfortable coming to him with bad news. However, he felt some team members with international backgrounds were not as comfortable sharing bad news with him. To overcome this, Henry developed a three-level system for raising concerns.

Level 1

A level 1 issue means that it is a known issue and the team are working on a solution. A level 1 issue only requires a subtle signal to the leader that the problem is under control and they do not need to be involved.

Level 2

A level 2 issue means the issue is known and there are different possible solutions. The team require the leader's feedback on which approach to take.

Level 3

A level 3 issue means there is a significant issue and the team are unsure how to proceed. The leader's support is required immediately.

By implementing this approach across the company, it creates two things. It means team members can save face with their leader because they can put distance between themselves and the issue at hand. Secondly, it prevents senior leaders from getting stuck on low-level problems, leaving more time to focus their efforts on more significant level 2 and level 3 issues.

CASE STUDY
LEVERAGING OPEN COMMUNICATION ACROSS A CALL CENTRE

James worked with highly skilled engineers, marketers and IT personnel to create new and exciting ways to solve customer problems. He was used to a fast-paced environment, where everyone was highly capable and professional in their approach.

He was keen to find a new challenge outside of this space to broaden his experience. As a result, he took on a role of managing a call centre that focused on providing customer service to the customers of their business-to-business products.

His new team consisted of staff in their early twenties, and casual or part-time employees — the opposite of his usual crew. The business had recently increased the pricing of their products, and most of the customers were not happy about it. As a result, James' customer service staff were being bombarded daily with negative feedback from customers. As a result, the team morale was dropping, and he knew he had to do something to change it.

On top of this, James' new boss was pushing him to make the team more productive as he felt they were not performing as well as they could, however, his boss did not outline what a productive team looked like.

Now, James was stuck with a team with reduced morale and productivity. Furthermore, he had no experience in this field and he was at a loss as to where to start.

He decided that the best way to turn things around was to create an open dialogue with the team, and this started with his direct reports. In his first meeting, he stated that he had no experience running a call centre and would be looking at each of them for advice and guidance. By showing vulnerability early, he quickly established trust among his direct reports. He explained that his background was in developing complex solutions and he lacked experience in call centres; however, he was keen to leverage his skills and the skills of the whole team to find solutions.

Once he felt he had built trust and respect with his direct reports, he focused on gathering feedback from the broader team. To facilitate open feedback across the group, he conducted a range of skip-level meetings. A skip-level meeting involves the leader meeting with the team members of their direct reports without their manager. Under the right conditions, these meetings can be an effective way to collect feedback that the team might be reluctant to provide in front of their manager. Keep in mind, this type of meeting needs to be managed carefully to prevent the direct reports feeling they are not trusted. The skip-level meetings provided James with a greater understanding of the team's roles, responsibilities and current challenges. It also became evident that staff were hesitant to provide open feedback due to fear of reprisal from their current managers.

Once James had gathered feedback from individual areas of the team, he needed to bring them together to develop a collective plan to improve the situation. The approach he adopted was to conduct a team retrospective: a strategy that aims to improve the performance of a team by providing both positive and constructive feedback.

Given this was the first time the team had undertaken such an approach, James wanted to make sure that the chosen strategy was easy to understand and allowed for the creation of actionable feedback. Knowing that there were low levels of trust between some staff and their line manager, he knew the staff would not provide the feedback required in an open forum. Also, research shows that when eliciting input from groups, it tends to create groupthink and the most vocal members get the most airtime.

As such, he asked each team member to anonymously write their thoughts on post-it notes across the following categories:

1. What is working?
2. What is not working?
3. What would you like to do differently?

By making this exercise anonymous, James was able to garner valuable feedback across all three areas. It also meant that every member of the team was able to provide suggestions and new ideas.

The group then discussed each category and developed themes. It soon became clear to everyone what was working, what was not working, and what they needed to do differently.

With a long list of required improvements and solutions, James did not want to dilute the team's efforts by trying to change too many areas at once. He decided to let the team vote on which ideas would have the most significant impact on their productivity and morale.

The team all agreed that the singular most significant factor holding them back was their ability to communicate ideas and issues openly. James knew the team would not switch overnight from not speaking their mind to confidentially airing their opinions. As such, the team decided the best way forward was to have an anonymous suggestion box in the group. Throughout the week, people could write their feedback on post-it notes and drop it into the box. At the end of each week, the entire team would review the post-it notes and determine which ideas would have an impact and who would implement them.

Concurrently, James worked with line managers to improve the relationship they had with their team. For some managers, this approach worked. Some managers, however, continued to resist the change, so James thought it best that they are moved out of the organisation.

Over the next two years, James actively focused on recruiting new leaders and staff members who communicated openly and honestly. He found that, as the level of trust in the team grew, they were more open to sharing new ideas. The productivity in the team also grew and the level of customer complaints steadily decreased. This was due to the growth in communication the team had developed, which had resulted in an ability to openly communicate with their customers the reasons for price or product changes.

THE LEADER SETS THE TONE

You set the tone for how transparent communication is across your team. It is critical through your interactions that you remain authentic. People can quickly ascertain when you are not genuine. This will erode the trust and respect you have worked hard to develop with your team.

The foundation of excellent communication is not speaking but listening. Active listening is a skill and, like any other skill, it requires practise and consistency to master it.

> **"GIVE PEOPLE THE TIME AND SPACE TO TALK WITHOUT YOU INTERRUPTING THEM."**

You might have found yourself in a situation where you are trying to talk to someone who is distracted and unfocused. If this happens repeatedly, you eventually give up trying to talk in these situations. Your team is more likely to come to you with their ideas, issues or thoughts if they know you will genuinely listen to them.

Active listening requires you to quieten your internal dialogue and focus on the person speaking to you without any distractions. You listen to their words, observe their body language and tone, and other non-verbal cues. Once you have mastered the art of listening, you are then more open to receive their meaning and provide constructive and timely feedback.

Before providing feedback, I always recommend that my clients ask for it first. By asking, you show you are vulnerable and open to receiving their feedback.

Ask your direct reports to provide feedback across two areas: what you are doing well and what can be improved. This ensures that you receive balanced and actionable feedback. You can do this in person or through a survey for people to provide feedback anonymously.

Another option is to ask people for observations on you and your leadership style. One of my clients would ask his executive assistant for feedback about his body language and other non-verbal cues when interacting with people. It was through this process that he uncovered he subconsciously crosses his arms over his chest in meetings. He realised he did this when people were providing feedback on his ideas. While he conveyed he was open to feedback, his body language was showing he was defensive.

Once you have established this method of receiving feedback, you can then leverage it to provide feedback to your team. This process also ensures that you provide your organisation with balanced feedback.

When providing feedback, always tackle the issue and never the person. Make sure feedback focuses on the topic and what can be done to fix it, rather than focusing on the person associated with that issue. For example, a client recently received feedback that one of her staff in the marketing team was having problems with the sales team. The sales team advised my client that they no longer liked working with this staff member. If she had passed this feedback onto the staff member, it would not have been useful as it would be personalising the issues. Instead, she spoke to the sales team to understand the specific issues they were having with the staff member from marketing. She uncovered that the sales team felt patronised when this staff member provided them with directives on how to sell products to their customers. Using this as a basis, she spoke to the staff member to determine her objective when advising the sales team on selling techniques for a specific product. She realised that this staff member was keen to get the sales team to sell the new products she was developing, and they were resistant. My client was able to make the staff member aware that her approach of pushing the sales team was not working. The staff member then had the feedback required to change her strategies. She explained to the sales team the importance of offering new products to customers, and they collectively agreed on a new sales target. She also decided not to get involved with the product sales process or approach.

UNDERSTAND HOW YOUR TEAM COMMUNICATES

Once you have established a practical approach to receiving and providing feedback, you should focus your efforts on uncovering how your team prefers to receive and absorb information. When it comes to communicating, one size does not fit all. An approach I used was to ask each direct report: how do you like to be informed?

While it is a simple question, it elicited a fruitful response. I had people tell me they prefer emails so they can review and digest, while others said they prefer a quick dot-point instant message. By understanding this, I was able to tailor my approach to each direct report.

I also asked them to identify what was getting in the way of us communicating effectively. For example, do they feel the communication methods are too complicated or is the communication not providing the right information? Conversely, you may be over-communicating. I have been in teams where so much information is continuously communicated that you end up opting out of reading or listening.

When considering communication with the broader team or organisation, you might want to develop a range of communication platforms. Like Dominic, who created a diverse range of interfaces from the weekly podcast and newsletter, to stand-up meetings and number-based reports. He was adamant that all staff could get the message and how they best wanted it received. Do not rely on monthly meetings, newsletters or worse, the annual performance review.

I asked Dominic what he would say to leaders who say they do not have time to communicate through these different forms. He told me that you make time for what is important to you and the business. Therefore, by prioritising open communication, you make time to make it work.

THE BOTTOM LINE — BALANCE OPEN COMMUNICATION AND TRUST

It is worth investing the time and effort in creating a team environment where open communication thrives. Research shows that it will lead to improvements in team performance and the company's financial results.

The strongest teams I have worked with clearly articulate the reasons behind significant decisions and solicit feedback from the team if it impacts them. Team members who had opportunities to provide feedback and understood the rationale behind the changes were more likely to support it. Leaders of these teams also ensure that when communicating significant changes, they aligned this to the team's purpose or company's purpose.

When trying to create open communication, remember to start with listening. By creating the space for active listening, you will show your team that you want and encourage ideas and feedback.

When starting on this journey, start small; you do not need to get communication departments or specialists involved to craft your message. Be authentic and tailor the communication in the preferred methods for individual team members or groups.

PRACTICAL ACTIVITY
DEVELOPING OPEN COMMUNICATION

ACTIVITY 1: CONDUCT YOUR RETROSPECTIVE MEETING

It is vital to use reviews to drive continuous improvement and learning. Retrospectives provide an opportunity to identify:

- What worked
- What did not work
- What can be improved
- What can be removed or avoided next time around.

Throughout my career, I have used different methodologies; however, the simplest and easiest way I learned was when working at REA Group, a publicly-listed market leading technology company.

The STOP, START, CONTINUE framework is a simple way of eliciting feedback from small to large groups of people.

The process is simple and powerful. I love that the approach can be used casually, in a one on one conversation over coffee to gain feedback. For example, whenever I take on a new leadership role, I always ask each direct report to tell me what areas we can Stop, Start and Continue in our business. I have also used it when facilitating groups of leaders to elicit feedback around their ways of working and how to change their work environment.

A simple approach I use when facilitating group conversations or team feedback is a large piece of paper with 'Start', 'Stop' and 'Continue' columns and a stack of sticky notes. Within each column, people write their observations about the 'Sprint' as they relate to the following categories:

Start: actions we should start taking
Stop: steps we should prevent or remove
Continue: activities we should keep doing and formalise

Table 3. Example of a STOP, START, CONTINUE table

STOP	START	CONTINUE
People turning up late	Limiting the agenda to the top three items to cover off	Attendees sending reading materials out 48 hours before the meeting
Using phones during meetings	Have everyone turn their phones on silent and place them face down on the table	Providing coffee
Having side conversations	Only one person speaks at a time	

This approach is an easy way to get started and does not feel too daunting if you or the team are not used to conducting reviews. It is also great if you are short on time or if your previous method of reviews was too time or labour intensive.

You will need to provide each participant with cards or post-it notes and a marker. Give them 10 minutes to write a single thought on each post-it notes under each of the three categories: Stop, Start, and Continue. It is essential to allow everyone to do this themselves. This prevents groupthink and allows the quieter members of the team to put their ideas forward.

Once finished, you can use three areas on a wall or sheet of paper to collect each point of feedback. Have a volunteer categorise the ideas under each group into a specific theme. Next, have the group share their thoughts and provide more detail for each of them. Take note of the ideas or processes that you want to continue. Then have the team vote on one or two ideas under the start and stop categories.

It is essential that you do not take on too many new ideas too quickly. It is also necessary that you remove processes or aspects of work that the whole team agree do not add value.

New ideas, insights or actions to create open communication across your team and business.

CHAPTER 9

TRAIT 6 – STRATEGIC FLEXIBILITY

Most leaders today know that nothing is guaranteed, and that change is the only constant. This uncertainty means they are continually making decisions which could fundamentally change the course of their business.

Flexibility on the job includes a willingness and ability to respond to changing circumstances and expectations readily. Being flexible when it comes to work is worth a lot. Employees who approach their job with a flexible mindset are typically more highly valued by employers.

The amount and speed of incoming information has outpaced most organisations' abilities to filter and determine which information is required to make effective decisions.

Whenever you mention flexibility at work, two things usually come to mind: the yoga class someone is teaching once a week in a meeting room and flexible hours; that is, I can come and go as required so that I can integrate work around my life.

My focus is neither of these areas. Instead, I will focus on the flexibility of goal approach and achievement. In my research,

I define this as 'The team was open to changing direction or approach when required.' I wanted the idea of flexibility to be relative to the team and the leader's organisational goals.

I have worked in a range of organisations, from ones where flexibility was the norm through to high command and control environments. I have also worked under managers who would provide specific directives (read: no flexibility) or, as we used to term it, the JDI – Just Do It.

The level of engagement (staff morale) in these teams was low and people were hesitant to go above and beyond to achieve the specific outcomes. Furthermore, over time, it meant that the teams became more reactive as they waited for the directives to flow down the chain of command before anyone would make the required decisions.

The flip side of that coin was working in the technology industry, where flexibility was the norm. Individual teams and their leaders had free reign to determine their goals and how they would tackle them. While this worked well most of the time, there were crucial projects that went well off track as people had too much flexibility and did not know what to do with it. Like a cat chasing the next shiny object, the goals kept changing. This resulted in time and money being wasted while chasing down ideas that did not align.

> **"WE CANNOT ALWAYS PREDICT WHEN CHANGE IS GOING TO HAPPEN; THAT IS WHY FLEXIBILITY IS SO IMPORTANT."**

When you are flexible, you are versatile, resilient and responsive to change. You can adapt to unexpected demands in the workplace: sudden surges in work, urgent problems, or an unpredictable event, such as a cybersecurity breach or a financial crash, for instance.

Flexibility works both ways and employees appreciate having flexible managers. Flexibility skills are also relevant to the approach management takes to handling employees. Flexible leaders treat employees as individuals and try to accommodate personal styles and needs.

Flexible leaders provide workers with considerable latitude about the way they accomplish goals. They assess the needs of employees and provide feedback, guidance, and recognition individually to optimise performance. Being flexible is beneficial for everyone.

The most significant benefit of flexible decision-making is speed, as a business who can identify and act upon opportunities quicker than their competitors will continue to grow and outperform others.

When this becomes an ingrained part of the culture, new ideas can come from any part of the organisation.

CASE STUDY
REMAINING FLEXIBLE IN A FAST-MOVING TECHNOLOGY BUSINESS

Jay is the head of a product development team for a top technology company in Australia. He and his team have the mandate to ensure that their products stay relevant in an ever-changing marketplace of major global technology companies.

Jay has a wealth of experience in product development and even ran his own technology start-up. In the past, Jay has relied on a more directive style of leadership. His method involved working closely with senior management to understand the company's broader strategy and translating that into critical pieces of work that his team could carry out.

While his style was sufficient, he found over time that it left little room for flexibility. The team had grown accustomed to taking their orders from him, and this lack of flexibility meant that Jay had, at some points in time, become a bottleneck for decision-making. This created delays which slowed down delivery of products to market.

When Jay started at the new technology company, he was expecting much of the same approach; however, he found this company operated very differently. Instead of issuing mandates or strategic directives, the leadership team would get together every quarter and set business priorities for the next 90 days. The company's view was that a 2- to 3-year strategic plan would stifle their ability to be flexible and seize opportunities as they arose.

Given this new context, Jay realised he too would have to adapt his leadership style. He needed to strike a balance between giving his team the flexibility to pursue new ideas and ensuring they hit the company objectives.

The first step in achieving this was to understand the capabilities of each team member and build a personal relationship based on trust. With this foundation in place, Jay set about developing a new way of working across the team.

For each business objective, he worked collaboratively with his team to define the ideal outcome they wanted and how they would track it (the key result). For example, the target for the quarter might be to drive usage rates on the app. The key results (metric) to track this was repeat users coming back to the app and time spent on the app per user.

With this objective and key result in mind, Jay left each individual and their respective teams to create a flexible approach to achieving it. To further encourage flexibility among his team and how they operated, they determined the purpose was to take risks and fail fast. This approach meant that they would take measured risks and get products out to customers quickly and thus, learn customer needs at a much faster pace. As a result, they were getting more products to market and gaining market feedback quicker than their competitors.

To ensure that flexibility did not result in teams chasing down the next shiny object, Jay also instituted what he called the 'four lenses to view an opportunity.' The teams had the flexibility to pursue new approaches and ideas if it met the following four criteria:

1. Can the customer use it?
2. Will the customer buy it?
3. Is it right for the overall business?
4. Can we build it?

Ideas or approaches that did not pass all four of these criteria were stopped. This focus ensured that each team had the flexibility to pursue new ideas but also stay focused on the company's purpose and goals.

To reinforce this new approach to flexibility, Jay also ensured the team celebrated when they achieved 50% of their stated outcome.

On the surface, this may sound strange: why celebrate if you did not achieve half of your goal? The purpose of this was to spur more significant innovation among the team. He found that teams that set more audacious goals (outcomes) had to be far more flexible in their approach to achieving it. This meant that they pushed themselves into new areas to learn and grow their capabilities.

The result was that Jay and his team sent more new products to market than ever before. It also meant that the team were learning more about consumers preferences quickly, and they could refine their product offering in less time.

THE BOTTOM LINE — FLEXIBLE DECISION-MAKING IMPROVES SPEED

To drive performance, flexible decision-making must be intrinsic in people's day-to-day ability to make decisions.

High-performance teams balance flexibility with effectiveness by providing safety barriers, to prevent distractions affecting their achievement of a goal.

In an ever-changing world, the key benefit of flexible decision-making is speed — companies which can seize opportunities faster than their competition will continue to grow.

PRACTICAL ACTIVITY
CREATING STRATEGIC FLEXIBILITY

1. FOCUS ON YOUR PURPOSE

Having key attributes that do not shift can keep you grounded during periods of change. Using your core values and your organisation's culture as anchor points will help you to decide what you can and cannot agree to when you receive an unexpected request.

2. BE OPEN MINDED

You will likely find it easier to understand and manage a situation if you look at it from a different perspective. For example, if you are looking to launch a new product, you might first like to analyse it from different viewpoints.

Such as:

- How will it fit into the marketplace?
- What will the impact be on the production process?
- How do you think the customers will react to it?

Make it a priority to listen to and understand the views of the other parties involved.

3. DEVELOP YOUR SKILL SET

If you do not try to learn new skills, you will likely find that when an unexpected event does occur, you will not be equipped to deal with it.

Tackle this by staying curious about what is going on around you. Keep up-to-date with new industry trends by reading up on the latest innovations and research and broaden your knowledge by cross-skilling.

4. BE OPTIMISTIC

It can be challenging to stay positive when you know a massive, urgent project is on the horizon. Looking on the bright side and focusing on the positives will help you to stay resilient and focused. A break or change in your routine could be an opportunity to learn new skills, or to work with different colleagues, new clients or new suppliers.

5. STAY CALM

When expectations shift suddenly, it can be disconcerting and you might find that you start to feel anxious. Counter the effects of stress (such as loss of focus and impaired decision-making) by taking steps to restore calm.

6. HAVE A STRONG SUPPORT NETWORK

Having a stable and robust team around you is essential in times of flux. It means that no matter the difficulties you are facing, you have people who you can rely on to support you.

Strengthen the relationships that you have with your co-workers by building trust. You could start by, for example, offering to take on additional tasks when a colleague is busy, or by helping him or her with a system or process that they are finding difficult to use.

New ideas, insights or actions to improve strategic flexibility.

CHAPTER 10

TRAIT 7 – EMPOWERMENT

Empowerment is the final stage in the evolution of a high-performance team. You have done it, and I commend you for staying on the journey.

A common question I am asked is: why is empowerment the final stage of a high-performance team's evolution and not addressed earlier?

Let me explain the rationale.

The foundation of a high-performance team is mutual trust and respect. Without trust and mutual respect in place, you cannot build a high-performance environment. Once you have this in place, together you can have frank conversations around what the purpose of your business is: What is the reason you exist? These discussions require soul searching and need everyone's input. You cannot achieve this level of commitment to a purpose without a healthy level of trust and mutual respect.

Once you have established your organisation's purpose, your focus is now defining roles and accountability. This helps each area of the organisation and its people to understand how they contribute to bringing the purpose to life each day. By setting expectations about responsibility, you create a sense of shared ownership across the business.

The next stage in the evolution of a high-performance business or team is ensuring that everyone communicates effectively and openly. As everyone is clear on the company's purpose and their roles and responsibilities, it becomes imperative that each area communicates effectively to achieve the company's goals.

In the last chapter, we focused on developing the business' strategic flexibility. Strategic flexibility is critical if the company is going to tackle the sheer volume of information and opportunities present in the modern marketplace.

It is only with all of these foundations in place that you, as a leader, can effectively empower your teams to achieve the company's goal.

Empowering your team without working on their ability to openly communicate, understanding their roles and accountabilities, or establishing a deep sense of trust and shared responsibilities, is a recipe for failure. That is because to be empowered, a team must know their direction, the objectives they need to achieve, the resources at their disposal, and how to communicate when issues inevitably arise.

My research defined empowerment as, 'The team had the authority to do what was needed to achieve the goals.' The concept is like autonomy; people had the sense that they could do what was needed.

THE JOURNEY TO TEAM EMPOWERMENT

An empowered company begins with self-empowerment. Empowerment is first and foremost a mindset shift in you. When I was working in large corporations, I treated every role and every department I led as my own business. Using this perspective, I would ask myself: if this were my money, how would I use it to have the most significant impact on my business? By looking at it as my own business, it also meant I empowered myself to make decisions today that would ensure the sustainability of the area for years to come. Not everyone I worked alongside, however, took this approach. Some managers would take significant risks, whereas others would always seek permission from the next manager in the chain of command.

At one point, I had a fantastic boss, Penny, who told me, "When in doubt, it is better to make the decision and seek forgiveness rather than permission." Under her guidance, the department I ran had the most successful year in acquiring new customer accounts in the past five years.

To be effective, a leader requires a solid understanding, not just of their area of business, but of human potential and self-esteem. It would help to work on yourself to understand the fears and barriers holding you back from playing big.

A common fear my clients have is: what if something goes wrong? or What if it all goes well and they do not need me anymore? Both of these questions, while on the surface seem sound, are coming from a place of fear. If you have asked yourself these questions at some point, I want you to pause and think: what was (is) driving these questions?

When most people consider failure, they think about top-level problems like bruised egos, embarrassment, or some form of reprimand.

If you are pushing your limits and taking risks, things will go wrong. Your focus should not be on things failing. Instead, it will help if you focus your efforts on what you will do when that happens.

PRACTICAL ACTIVITY
OVERCOMING FEAR

To help my clients overcome the fear of embarrassment or reprimand, I have them perform an activity called Drilling the Iceberg.

The first step is to take an A4 piece of paper and draw a line straight down the middle. On the left-hand side, you write what happens when something fails; for example, my boss will be mad. Then write down what you think may happen next. The key is to keep writing down each fear. Like a domino effect, they do tend to get worse and worse. The client usually ends up in a dark place created by their underlying concerns.

I then direct them to go to the top of the right-hand side of the page and start writing down what plans or countermeasures they would put in place to combat each fear. For example, the countermeasure of 'my boss will get mad' is advising my boss upfront of the possible risks and plans to rectify. You repeat this process for each of your fears. Then against each fear and accompanying countermeasure, you list the probability of the problem escalating now that you have these new measures in place.

The process works because it involves applying rational thought to irrational fear.

Now that you have tackled your fears to empower yourself, you are ready to start empowering others around you. By empowering your team, you are freeing yourself up to take on bigger goals and challenges for the organisation. Also, it gives you the space to evolve your leadership style to focus on maximising the organisation's and the team's potential rather than managing workload.

On the following page is a table showing common fears that people may have when presenting their ideas to their boss and peers for feedback (Table 4).

In this instance, the fears are listed on the left-hand side. You will see that the real underlying fear is not the presentation itself but the ramifications of getting it wrong. You will notice that by developing countermeasures and actions, each fear can be tackled to prevent a runaway train.

Table 4. Fears and Countermeasures

Fear	Countermeasure
The boss will ask me a tough question during my presentation.	Prepare for possible questions ahead of time that might get asked.
	Give my boss an outline of the presentation and ask for any questions.
	Prepare a holding statement for tough questions, such as "Good question. I will need to look into that and get back to you."
The boss will think that I have no idea what I am doing	Speak to the boss and ask for feedback, specifically two things I did well and one area I can improve on.
The boss will start taking work away from me because they do not trust my abilities.	Be upfront with my boss and ask what has driven the change in workload.
The rest of the business thinks I am bad at my job.	
The boss fires me because I cannot do my job properly.	
I cannot find another job.	
I lose my house.	

GETTING EMPOWERMENT RIGHT

Accountability, support and knowledge form the backbone of effective empowerment. Would you let an untrained driver drive your car?

> **"IN BUSINESS, PEOPLE ASSUME THAT EMPOWERMENT MUST BE AN ALL-OR-NOTHING GAME."**

People may bypass building the foundations outlined in the previous chapters, but each of the earlier traits is essential to creating an environment where individuals and teams can be empowered. Empowerment is the last stage of the High-Performance Team Model (Figure 3, page 37).

The first step to empowering your team is gauging their appetite for it. For example, some people might prefer high levels of autonomy, whereas others would prefer lower levels. You need to tailor the level of empowerment for each team member based on a conversation with them and deep understanding of their skills, capabilities, willingness to learn and self-confidence.

This should be an ongoing conversation you are having with your team, not a once off. As people grow more confident and capable in their skills, they might seek more autonomy. Conversely, giving a highly-confident, low-skilled employee empowerment could lead to putting them and the company at unnecessary risk. The risk here is that employees who are overly confident and low-skilled tend not to listen to other people's advice.

The same can be said for highly-skilled employees who fail to see their own limitations, thus having a misplaced sense of empowerment in certain situations. To give an example of this, I recall one day in the office when a colleague collapsed. He was conscious but having severe chest pains. Luckily, two staff on the floor were first aid trained and went to provide help. They were stopped by a woman in a more senior position. She kept demanding that, as the most senior person on the floor, she should manage the situation – despite limited training or knowledge in first aid. Luckily for my colleague, the work colleagues with first aid training eventually prevailed and provided the required aid until an ambulance arrived.

Unable to see her own misplaced empowerment, the woman later made a formal complaint to human resources about the first aiders lack of respect for her role. The risks of misplaced empowerment mentioned above occur when the previous traits have not been cemented into the team culture. In instances like these, the leader will need to revisit ways of developing a trusting and respectful environment involving open communication, accountability and flexibility.

Empowering members of an organisation is a tremendous, motivational tool. It allows team members to contribute to improving performance and achieving better results. Empowered staff are loyal, committed and potentially more productive. By giving the team the tools and resources needed to successfully manage or lead their projects, work towards their goals and drive their career, the benefits are endless.

My research has found that team members who feel empowered in their roles are more likely to:

- go the extra mile
- follow best practices
- be more productive
- have good communication
- embrace change
- have a 'can-do' attitude
- provide better customer service.

If your business is geographically spread, such as retail or multinationals, empowering local staff will give them the confidence to adopt strategies and approaches to the local conditions and enable them to respond quickly to change.

CASE STUDY
DRIVING EMPOWERMENT IN A REGULATED INDUSTRY

Brooke is a senior leader in the retail energy market. Retail energy is a highly-regulated and compliance-driven market. There are many rules and laws that govern how to conduct businesses in this sector.

The heavy focus on compliance naturally seeps into the broader culture of the organisation. It means most leaders are hesitant to empower their people for fears that something could go wrong, and worst case, a compliance breach. Depending on the severity, a compliance breach could result in hefty fines for the organisation and staff reprimands or dismissal.

When Brooke took on her new role — leading a new marketing team — she already faced her first big challenge. She had sixteen vacant positions and only three roles filled. On top of this, she had steep targets to achieve in little time and the business was looking to her for a new way of marketing.

Brooke knew then that she would not be able to follow the traditional approach to management: try and manage everything yourself and surround yourself with "doers".

To drive a step-change across marketing, she needed to hire people with problem-solving abilities, a can-do attitude and technical skills.

Brooke knew that an approach like this would be contentious and might rock the boat with other managers across the organisation. As a result, she openly communicated her strategy with her boss and her peers. By openly communicating the new approach and taking full accountability — knowing that it was a radical approach for such a highly compliance-driven organisation — she was able to tackle people's concerns and get her leader's support.

Brooke set forth and intentionally sought through her network and referrals to create a shortlist of people who were deemed as domain experts. She then took the unusual step of hiring these people without providing a finalised position description. Instead, she spent two full days with each new hire, helping them understand the company's purpose, values and the regulatory environment. She also used this time to build trust and mutual respect. At the end of the two days of intensive sessions, the new hire gained vital knowledge of the company, expectations of their role, and an understanding of how their position was contributing to delivering the company's purpose.

Brooke took the extraordinary step of having the new hire create and finalise their role. Co-creating their role was their first taste of empowerment. By Brooke creating 70% and clearly articulating the compliance requirements, the new hire was free to develop the remainder. Their job was to craft the remaining 30% based on their understanding of the company's goal and purpose, and their expert knowledge of their field. She was determined to hire people who were highly skilled in their respective areas and then give them the power to achieve the organisation's goals.

Once the team member was on board and felt secure in the organisation, Brooke moved onto the next phase, which was delegating. Now, unlike traditional delegation models whereby managers hand down work that they do not want to do themselves or find beneath them, Brooke took a fresh approach by asking every individual these questions:

1. How is your current workload?
   Brooke was trying to ascertain how quickly each new member of her team was settling into the work. Brooke established that they were comfortable and competent.
2. What are you comfortable taking on?
   The purpose of this question was to understand what additional work they would be willing to take on based on their capacity, skill set and the current business needs.
3. How can I best support you?

Her approach of using open-ended questions is an excellent avenue for honest conversation. This helped her gauge the individual needs and desires of each team member. It also meant that she could dial up or down the level of work to ensure everyone was working at their peak.

As a result, Brooke was able to create a continuum of delegation. As her team's confidence grew, Brooke progressively put them into more significant projects or development opportunities that would improve their capabilities. The process meant that she was steadily building on the initial levels of trust she established during the first two days.

Now, this is not to say that it was all smooth sailing. There were times when budgets were overrun, and marketing campaigns did not achieve their targets. However, by making the failures manageable, both she and her team members knew the risks.

Brooke never saw these situations as failures. Instead, she would ask herself, 'What could I have done differently?' and would ask her team, 'What could you have done differently?' By instilling a sense of shared accountability, she was able to develop her team further. Also, the team were able to trust her even more knowing that failure was an opportunity for them both to learn. Her approach turned what could have been a confidence-deflating moment into one for learning.

The result was that she was able to drive a new level of thinking across the marketing department and the team's engagement score increased to 81% – one of the highest across the organisation.

For her, it meant that she had more time to think about the future of the business and how she could position it to capitalise on the changing needs of consumers.

CASE STUDY
EMPOWERMENT AT A LEGAL START-UP

Marianne is the founder of a multi-award winning legal firm, Legal Lite. The purpose of her firm sounds simple: for clients to love their lawyer. Now, in most instances, when you think of lawyers, love is not the first word to mind. Marianne was determined to change that.

Marianne spent the first decade of her career training at a large law firm. After a time of feeling like a number, she decided to move onto a role in a medium-sized firm, and then took a position in a boutique firm. Unfortunately, the situation was always the same. The firms changed in size, but the way they operated and managed their people was still the same.

Marianne came to realise that if she wanted to change the industry, she would have to do it herself. So, she developed Legal Lite, a law firm that does not use traditional practices, such as hourly billing or set targets for staff to bring in a specific amount of revenue.

During her time in other law firms, Marianne had witnessed poor management of sexism, bullying, and a lack of respect and trust, all demonstrating a lack of care for staff as people. She saw first-hand the impact this was having on people's mental health and well-being. Starting her firm, she made this non-negotiable. She told me that as a leader, looking after people's well-being is critical.

When she started the firm, she assumed it would be a low-key business, and she would be the sole practitioner. However, the market responded exceptionally well to her fresh approach, and within three months, she hired her first employee. Hiring an employee meant she had to start thinking more about her leadership style and approach.

Initially, she focused on doing the opposite of what she experienced in other law firms. This approach worked for a while; however, as her firm grew, she knew she would have to focus more on developing herself and her approach to leadership.

Marianne describes her leadership style as 'very empowering.' What this means in practical terms is that she does not tell her staff what to do. Instead, she involves them in the decision-making process from the start. For example, instead of having traditional annual performance reviews, Marianne has a one-on-one meeting with each team member once a month. During this meeting, they discuss performance, positive and constructive feedback, and goals for the next month. An essential part of this conversation is providing her staff with strategic flexibility to set their objectives for the month ahead. She then focuses on providing the right level of support and accountability to achieve these goals.

But not everything turns out how you expect it, so when things go wrong, the focus is not on finding who was at fault. The process focuses on acknowledging there is a problem and how best to fix the problem. The key to ensuring issues do not arise is ensuring staff are empowered by knowing there are quality assurance checks in place. For example, I always check document drafting or legal advice before it goes out, but I do trust my staff to handle email enquiries, phone calls and do the initial draft and follow-ups.

When things go wrong, Marianne tackles this upfront by providing timely and constructive feedback. Instead of pointing the finger or blaming staff, she takes a more collaborative approach based on asking questions rather than telling. For example, she would ask: How do you think you went on this project? In most instances, people know when they have fallen short of their own or the firm's standards.

Marianne tells me that using this approach has meant staff feel empowered to handle the projects how they see fit. More impressive is that to date, there have been no surprises in performance in both Marianne or her staff; everyone always knows where they stand.

Marianne's approach to empowerment is intuitive and useful. Her advice is to go gradually and to customise a plan to each team member's skill set, experience and personality. It is important to understand each team member's nature, how much they can do, and what types or complexity of projects they can take on. When this information is established, spend time in the onboarding and initial stages to provide them with the right training. To make sure they understand their role and how it fits within the organisation, be clear on expectations, especially around the standards of work. Once past these initial stages, Marianne makes sure they receive timely feedback and ongoing support.

She describes the process as learning to ride a bike: You start wobbly with training wheels and then, over time, you can ride free.

THE BOTTOM LINE – EMPOWERMENT IS A MOTIVATIONAL TOOL

To empower your team, you first need to let go of your fears and embrace that, when done correctly, it will lead to a higher level of performance for yourself and your team.

When introducing empowerment, start small and take managed risks.

Be clear on the expectations and let your team know you are there to support them and to help them manage the risks. By providing psychological safety, your team are more likely to focus on achieving their goals rather than avoiding failure.

View empowerment as a continuum whereby the level of empowerment provided is continuously adjusted based on the company's and the team's needs. In the end, however, the buck will stop with you as the leader. So, use the opportunity when things go wrong to reflect and ask yourself, 'What could I have done differently to support them to succeed?'

PRACTICAL ACTIVITY
CREATING AN EMPOWERED TEAM

Here are steps you can take today to help your team feel empowered:

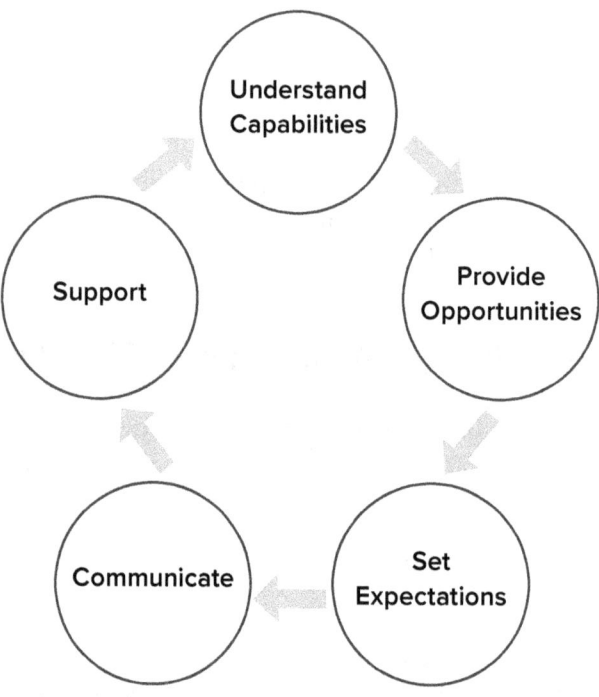

Figure 10. Empowerment Cycle

STEP 1: UNDERSTAND EACH TEAM MEMBER'S CAPABILITIES AND DEVELOPMENT AREAS

Speak to each of your direct reports individually to understand their specific skill sets, capabilities and areas they want to develop. If you do regular performance reviews and development plans, this understanding will be an excellent foundation for these conversations.

STEP 2: PROVIDE OPPORTUNITIES FOR OWNERSHIP

Make a list of all the tasks or activities that you do regularly. Go through this list and highlight which activities you could effectively delegate to someone in your team. For example, if a team member wants to get better at public speaking, you might delegate to them a regular meeting where they need to present.

If you dread specific tasks such as building financial models and a member of your team enjoys it, you could delegate this task to them. Let a team member take on a new project — and run with it. When you delegate different (even small) tasks to an employee, it empowers them to get the job done, and done well.

STEP 3: SET EXPECTATIONS AND GUIDELINES

When team members understand their expectations, the guidelines they are to work within and know which boundaries they can push, they can do their job more effectively and feel more supported. It is also critical that you both agree on a successful outcome. You might want to set measures for success, as well as gather subjective feedback, including feedback from other stakeholders or the team around how it went.

STEP 4: ENCOURAGE COMMUNICATION

Empowerment does not mean you are silent throughout the process. It is essential that you and the team member communicate regularly. Ideally, determine upfront the right level of communication. This will prevent your team from feeling that you are micromanaging them by over-communicating.

STEP 5: OFFER SUPPORT

Individual or team coaching to identify road roadblocks, find solutions and then act can be extremely helpful; however, always ask permission before providing it. Your team will develop by learning from their successes and their mistakes. If you step in too early to prevent failure, you might miss a critical learning opportunity for them.

New ideas, insights or actions for creating an empowered team.

PART III
ACHIEVING HIGH PERFORMANCE

CHAPTER 11

IMPLEMENTING THE HIGH-PERFORMANCE TEAM MODEL

So far, you have learned about the barriers to creating a high-performance team and the seven traits which consistently lead to high performance. The following is a case study based on real-world implementation of the High-Performance Team Model in the workplace.

CASE STUDY
CREATING A HIGH-PERFORMANCE COMMERCIAL SALES TEAM

Kylie worked for the owner of some of Australia's largest shopping centres. During her time, she had made a name for herself as a level-headed, reliable and ambitious salesperson. She knew how to strike the right deal that met both her clients' and business' objectives. The company recognised her talents and offered her the new role of leading a sales team of six people. They also gave her charge of two of their most important shopping centres. One was performing well, and they held ambitious growth plans.

The other was in a prime location but struggling to secure retailers and therefore the foot traffic was dwindling.

I was brought in to provide Kylie with executive coaching when she was already six months into the new role. From our initial coaching session, it was clear she was eager to develop her leadership capabilities; however, she was acutely aware that she needed her and her new team to achieve their sales targets.

The desire to develop and deliver is not surprising. No one operates in a vacuum where the company allows them to develop their skills without pressure to achieve the key results. I explained to Kylie that coaching is not something that happens to you. Instead, it is a partnership where you need to be willing to put in the work to develop new skills and a positive mindset to drive continuous success. As humans, we need to view ourselves as a constant work in progress. Coaching accelerates this work, but you need to understand you are never finished.

To commence the program, we benchmarked Kylie and her team using our high-performance team benchmarking tool. This tool provides a business or team with an overview of their operations within the seven traits of high-performance and identifies areas that need attention. Kylie and I needed the unvarnished view of how she and the team were performing in each of the high-performance team behaviours (Figure 11).

Working with Kylie, we identified two areas she wanted to focus on. These areas were chosen as they would have the most significant impact on performance. Her initial thoughts were that, as the team was very structured in terms of the sales portfolio each person managed, and the way they worked, there was little room to improve. She decided she wanted to focus on open communication and creating a deep sense of purpose across the team.

To create a more profound sense of purpose, we explored what purpose in the role meant for both Kylie and her team. The previous manager of the team had assumed that, given the team were leasing retail spaces in shopping centres, their purpose was clear – to get more businesses to rent shop space.

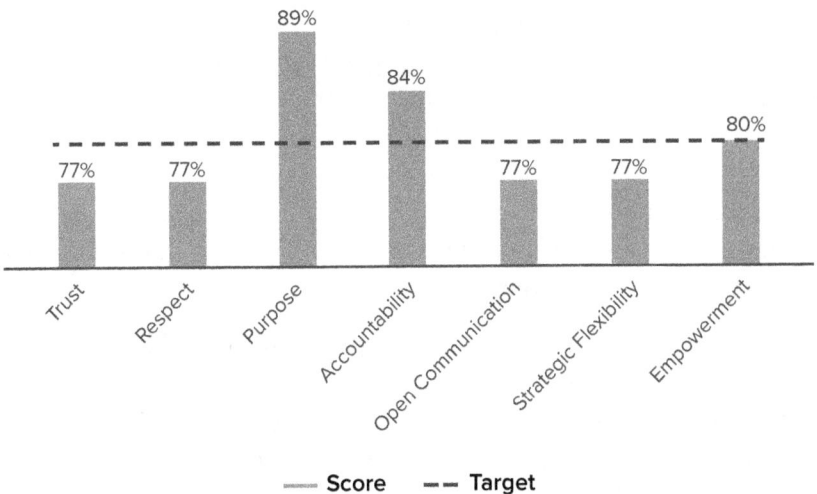

Figure 11. High-Performance Team Coaching Program Implementation Scores (Pre-intervention)

Matching retailers with available space did not resonate with Kylie. Given the high staff turnover in the team before taking over, she suspected it did not resonate with them either.

After some guided reflection during our coaching sessions, Kylie realised that her purpose for being in the role was to help retail businesses succeed. She had always had a keen interest in the commercial retail estate and retail business from a young age. She had also experienced downturns and the heartache of seeing small retailers over-committing to long leases and having to close.

Once she was clear on why she wanted to remain in this role and succeed, she proceeded to discuss her passion individually with each of her team members. Through this process, she discovered that many of them shared a passion for various forms of retail: from food and technology through to high-end fashion brands.

Kylie also discovered that one of her team did not share this passion. The staff member was finding it draining to be out meeting potential retailers and meeting their demands consistently. It was through this conversation that the team member realised that, while she had a passion for sales, she was not passionate about commercial space or retailing. Over the next four weeks, Kylie helped this team member find her passion, which was account management for technology products. Using this, she made introductions to her contacts in this space and helped the team member find a role outside the organisation that was more suited to her passions and talents.

Through collective brainstorming, the remaining team decided on a purpose statement – being a trusted partner to new and established retailers to drive their success. With a renewed sense of purpose in place, we shifted our focus to creating defined roles and accountabilities.

Kylie worked with her team to determine how well each of their roles and responsibilities aligned with their purpose. Each member was then assigned a portfolio such as fashion, consumer electronics and ladies accessories. Along with each portfolio came specific sales targets they needed to achieve. She discovered that two members of the team were not passionate about their assigned portfolios. One would prefer to work with food retailers, and the other wanted to focus on high-end fashion brands. Kylie shifted the roles and provided them with their preferred portfolios. Kylie saw an almost immediate shift in their attitudes and subsequent results.

By aligning people to their natural passions and giving them the responsibility to ensure these shops succeeded, sales staff became proactive in hunting down new retailers who would fit the individual centre's demographics and trends. As opposed to reactively placing retailers in the most prominent available spaces, they let them move into a smaller space for twelve months. They agreed with the retailer that if demand remained high after twelve months, they would look to place them into a larger area. Even though the business earned less in the short term, it minimised the risks for the retailer for starting a new business. The new partnership approach was helping to shift the perception of the sales team from commercial real estate agents to trusted partners.

Having established roles and responsibilities aligned to the team's purpose, we shifted our focus to improving the level of mutual respect among the team. The team's feedback was that Kylie was always a respectful leader. However, there were issues with how some members of the team changed their behaviour when she was not present. 'When the cat is away, the mice will play,' the saying goes.

Based on the make-up of Kylie's team, two members were the most vocal. As a result, the other team members did not put forward their views for fear of it being rejected publicly. We needed an approach that would enable the quieter members of the group to put forward their ideas. To achieve this, I encouraged her to work closely with each team member to identify what a respectful work environment looked like to them. This approach ensured that each team member was able to voice their opinions and ideas openly.

From there, Kylie gathered the team to determine a list of behaviours that make up a respectful work environment. Kylie's role in this discussion was not to lead but to sit back, observe and facilitate. It was critical that the team felt they had developed the resolution, as it would be the team that held each other accountable.

After each member had shared their ideas, the group voted on three new behaviours they believed a high-performance team would exhibit. I recommended they limited themselves to three actions as this was unchartered territory for them, and it would take some time for everyone to adapt to the change in behaviours.

Behavioural change is always tricky. Once the initial motivation to change wears off, people quickly slide into their old behaviours. To tackle this, Kylie and I helped the team develop a set of strategies for how they would handle it if a team member or Kylie were not exhibiting these behaviours.

The team took a two-pronged approach. Step one was to have the conversation one-on-one with the team member and make them aware of their behaviours and how it impacted the team.

This gave the team member the opportunity to make amends for their behaviour. If the practice continued, then it would be raised with Kylie for her to address directly. The team also agreed that they would provide timely feedback to Kylie if they felt she was not leading by example.

As a result, the mood in the team improved dramatically, and Kylie found that all team members openly shared ideas. She also found the team became comfortable debating new ideas and building on each other's ideas to find the right outcome.

One team member, however, refused to change their behaviours despite ongoing support. After three months of various interventions, they were asked to leave the company. While this was not the intention from the outset, it sent the message that Kylie or the team would not tolerate disrespectful behaviour.

With these foundation pieces in place, we focused our efforts on how Kylie communicated with her team. Upon deep reflection, she realised she had been using a method with her team that she had enjoyed when working with her previous managers.

I coached Kylie to think about her communication preferences. I then asked each team member what their communication preferences were and how Kylie should best adapt her style. She received productive feedback with some members liking her direct manner, however, others preferred to obtain essential information in writing so that they could ponder and respond. Also, other members of the team preferred to talk through their problems or ideas openly and use Kylie as a sounding board. It came as a surprise to hear that, in a team of six direct reports, they would have such varied communication preferences. We tend to communicate based on our preferred style. For example, assume you need to find out some information from a colleague. People who tend to verbalise their thoughts will call and usually say something like, 'I thought it would be easier to chat about this over the phone.' In comparison, someone else who prefers time to formulate an idea or ponder a suggestion might send an email. We assume that people want to be communicated in the same way that we do, but these differing preferences should be taken into account when communicating with staff.

Based on this feedback, I worked with Kylie to restructure her standard one-on-one meetings. Before the coaching, Kylie would meet each team member for one hour once a week to discuss their portfolio and sales targets. Based on the feedback, she tailored the meetings to suit each person's preferred communication style. For example, for some team members she would send a dot point agenda 24 hours before their session and ask them to do the same. For other staff members, she would walk through the centre so they could visit the sales representative customers and discuss ideas and obstacles. Finally, for the two members who wanted more empowerment, she cancelled the regular catch-up. She advised them to see her whenever they needed support.

It took approximately six months to embed and ensure the team adopted the new behaviours. From there, it was time to focus on the pinnacle of a high-performance team—empowerment.

Through coaching, Kylie was able to identify the key strengths, development areas and level of empowerment each team member was comfortable having at any given time. Given the nature of their roles, she initially felt limited with how to empower the team. Through discussion, we came up with a range of strategies. For more experienced staff, she enables them to develop their own sales plans and target customers based on their insights and market trends.

She worked with the less experienced staff to develop sales plans and targets but let them handle all their customer meetings themselves without her supervision. By tailoring her approach to balance the individual's objectives and the company's goals, she was able to ensure everyone felt trusted to achieve their outcomes.

At this point, I conducted another High-Performance Team Assessment for both Kylie and her team. I was keen for Kylie to see the impact the changes she had made had on herself and her team (Figure 12).

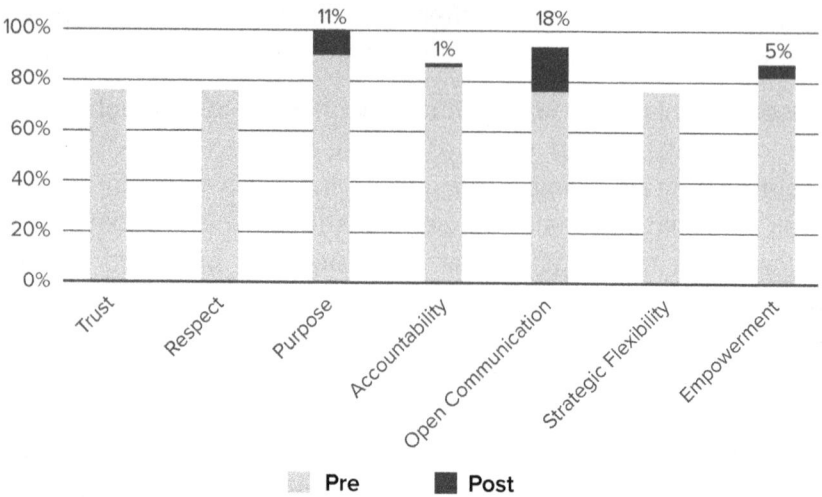

Figure 12. High-Performance Team Coaching Program Implementation Scores (Post-intervention)

You will notice that the two key areas of focus – Purpose and Open Communication – dramatically improved.

DEVELOPING AN ACTION PLAN

Remember, to create a high-performance team, you need to master the seven traits – trust, respect, purpose, accountability, open communication, strategic flexibility and empowerment. These traits have been shown to drive high performance across different industries and team sizes, as you have read from the case studies. It is imperative when developing a high performance team that you do not try and change everything at once. You need to determine which traits will have the most significant impact for you, your team and your business and focus on them. It is for this reason that you need an ACTION PLAN.

The plan aims to identify the type of behavioural change you are seeking, and then formulate a plan to achieve that behavioural change. The plan should include strategies to implement measurable benchmarks and consider possible barriers and ways to overcome them. It will also help to identify the benefits such change will have on the business, and the rewards for you, your team, or your business once the behavioural change has been achieved.

There is a High-Performance Team Action Plan worksheet on page 179, which will guide you through the considerations to make on your way to achieving a high-performance team. Before developing your plan to move forward, let's recap what you have learned.

To generate high-performance consistently across a business, you need to build an environment for people to thrive. The High-Performance Team Model outlines the critical building blocks – the seven traits – that are required to create teams which strive for high-performance.

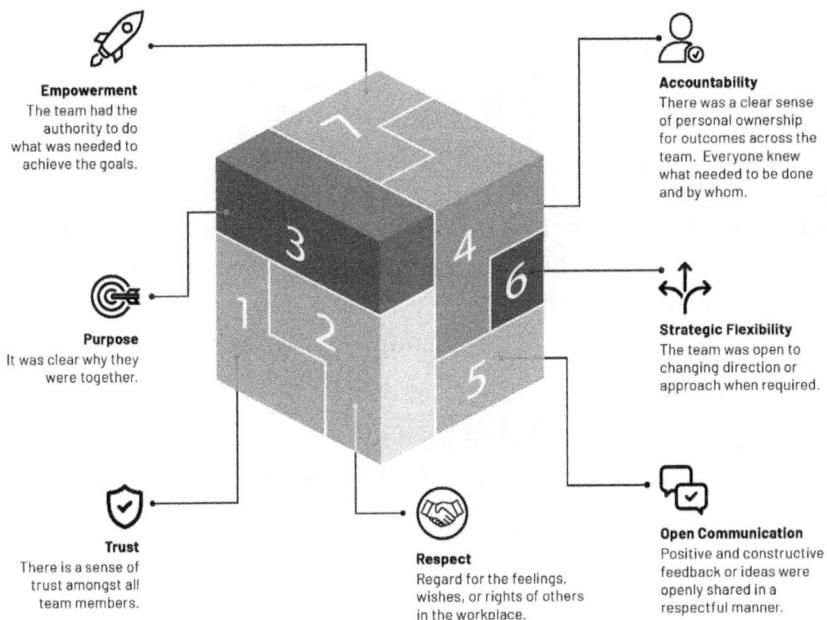

Empowerment
The team had the authority to do what was needed to achieve the goals.

Accountability
There was a clear sense of personal ownership for outcomes across the team. Everyone knew what needed to be done and by whom.

Purpose
It was clear why they were together.

Strategic Flexibility
The team was open to changing direction or approach when required.

Trust
There is a sense of trust amongst all team members.

Respect
Regard for the feelings, wishes, or rights of others in the workplace.

Open Communication
Positive and constructive feedback or ideas were openly shared in a respectful manner.

Figure 13. High-Performance Team Model (HPTM)

Let's recap the seven traits:

Trait 1: Trust

Your actions – not words – build trust.

Trust is like a joint bank account held between you and your team. Every day your actions and the teams' actions can go towards building more trust. Trust is the solid foundation from which all other behaviours are developed. High levels of trust ensure the organisation thrives in easy and challenging times.

Behaviours to adopt to develop trust are:

1. Be vulnerable
2. Take care of people's well-being
3. Give credit
4. Keep your promises
5. Be transparent

Trait 2: Respect

Respect is a powerful force.

In workplaces with high levels of respect, people share ideas, constructively disagree with each other, and seek to understand each other's perspectives. Each of these qualities enable the team to deliver the best outcomes. These behaviours will also transcend beyond the company's walls and flow into how the company treats its customers, suppliers and the communities in which they operate.

The four-step model (Figure 6, page 69), shows the actions a leader can take to create a respectful environment:

- Step 1: Set Clear Expectations
- Step 2: Be a role model
- Step 3: Reinforce positive behaviour and correct disrespectful behaviours
- Step 4: Embed this into your ways of working

Trait 3: Purpose
A sense of purpose benefits all.

Having a clear purpose can drive strategic clarity, transformation and innovation, as well as improving relationships both inside and outside the organisation.

The benefits of a clear purpose impact positively across all areas of a business and team, such as staff morale, strategy implementation, innovation and profits.

To help you define a clear purpose, you had the opportunity to create an Ikigai, a Japanese approach to finding what is important to you (Figure 8, page 86). Review this now — would you make any amendments to this purpose after reading more?

Trait 4: Accountability
Role clarity ensures accountability.

High levels of accountability are critical to the performance of successful teams. Leaders of these teams benefit from higher levels of employee participation, increased commitment of team members to their work and staff morale. There is also an increased levels of innovation and creativity.

By aligning an individual's role to the team's and the company's purpose, you help people become accountable, as they feel they belong to something larger than just their function.

To operate at a high level, you need to remove the ambiguity and be clear about people's roles and responsibilities. To drive accountability across your team, four activities were presented:

- Activity 1: Aligning roles to your purpose
- Activity 2: Creating clear position descriptions
- Activity 3: Defining Decision-Making Authorities
- Activity 4: The 50% rule

Trait 5: Open Communication

Balance open communication and trust.

A high-performance team communicates openly, promptly and with the intent that the feedback and ideas improve the performance of the organisation. There is also a definitive link between open communication and financial performance.

Open communication succeeds when the leader sets the tone and actively provides and seeks feedback. Retrospective meetings are a way of quickly gathering quality feedback from your team as they offer the opportunity to identify:

- what worked
- what did not work
- what can be improved
- what can be removed or avoided next time around

The STOP, START, CONTINUE framework is a simple way of eliciting feedback.

Trait 6: Strategic Flexibility

Flexible decision-making improves speed.

Flexibility includes the willingness and ability to respond to changing circumstances and expectations readily. Employees who approach their careers with a flexible mindset are typically more highly valued by employers.

To drive performance, flexible decision-making must be intrinsic in people's day-to-day ability to make decisions. High-performance teams balance flexibility with effectiveness by providing safety barriers around it, that prevents distractions from affecting their achievement of a goal. The key benefit of flexible decision-making is speed.

To create a strategically flexible workplace, you must:

1. Focus on your purpose
2. Be open-minded
3. Develop your skill set
4. Be optimistic
5. Stay calm
6. Have a strong support network

Trait 7: Empowerment

Empowerment is a motivational tool.

Empowerment is the final stage in the evolution of a high-performance team. To empower your team, you first need to let go of your fears and embrace that, when done correctly. Empowerment will lead to a higher level of performance for yourself and your team.

When starting with empowerment, start small and take managed risks. Be clear on the expectations and let your team know you are there to support them and help them manage the risks. By providing psychological safety, your team is more likely to focus on achieving their goals rather than avoiding failure.

View empowerment as a continuum whereby the level of empowerment provided is continuously adjusted based on the company's and the team member's needs. Use the opportunity when things go wrong to reflect and ask yourself: What could I have done differently?

There are five steps to creating an empowered team:

1. Understand each member's capabilities and development areas
2. Provide opportunities for ownership
3. Set expectations and guidelines
4. Encourage communication
5. Offer support

HIGH-PERFORMANCE TEAM ACTION PLAN

Consider each of the questions below before creating your action plan on the following page. The action plan is also available online at: bareinc.com.au.

1. Which high-performance behavioural trait will I focus on achieving?
2. What observable change(s) in behaviour do I want to see?
3. How will I measure the effectiveness of the change? Examples: The number of new ideas shared at every team meeting or the number of times team members give and receive feedback.
4. When do I want to achieve this behavioural change?
5. What are the benefits for me of making this behavioural change?
6. What are the benefits for my team of making this behavioural change?
7. What are the benefits for my company of making this behavioural change? These benefits could be across some or all the following areas:
   - personal
   - professional
   - financial (profit, revenue, cost)
   - time (reduced downtime, increased speed to market)
   - customer satisfaction
8. What are the top three things that could stop me from achieving this change?
9. What solutions can I implement to overcome these challenges?
10. How will I engage my team?
11. How will I monitor our progress?
12. How will I support myself when I do not exhibit this new behaviour?
13. How will I support my team when they do not exhibit this new behaviour?
14. How will I reward myself and the team for achieving this change?

The High-Performance Team Action Plan

Trait:

Description:

Success Metrics:

When:

Benefits		
Myself	**Team**	**Company**
1.	1.	1.
2.	2.	2.
3.	3.	3.

Implementation	
Challenges	**Solutions**
1.	1.
2.	2.
3.	3.

Team Engagement:

Monitoring Progress:

Support:

Reward:

CONCLUSION

I want you to imagine what it would mean for you and the company to harness the potential of all team members. What would it do for your bottom line and engagement levels if everyone in your business put in a little more each day?

At the start of this book, I promised you I would dispel the misconception that the top 20% of the organisation drives high performance. Similarly, I wanted to remove the idea that merely having a strategy would be enough to create a high-performance business or team. Your strategy is executed by your most significant asset: your people. You do not need to offer fancy perks or be a well-known brand to drive high performance. The case studies in this book have come from a range of businesses – from start-ups to well-known brands – each who are driving high performance their way.

As a leader, you have a range of resources available to achieve your goals. The most significant impact; however, will be achieved by spending time and energy on cultivating the development of your team. For you to flourish as a leader, you need to have a team that can handle the challenges and opportunities that are thrown at them every day.

When you have a capable team, you are freed to focus your mind on the broader strategic questions, such as how to continue evolving your business to ensure that it remains relevant and profitable in our ever-changing marketplace.

I hope that you found this book both informative and practical. Use this book as a blueprint for you to build your high-performance team. It is through the implementation of the High-Performance Team Model, and with you as the custodian that we will drive positive change.

If you want to continue learning from other high-performance leaders, please sign up to my newsletter at bareinc.com.au, where I share more insights.

> **"UNLESS SOMEONE LIKE YOU CARES A WHOLE AWFUL LOT, NOTHING IS GOING TO GET BETTER. IT'S NOT."**
> — DR SEUSS, THE LORAX

As leaders, we are always faced with challenges and wins; however, it is leaders like you that care a whole awful lot that will drive the change in your organisation and the broader society.

For that, I will always be grateful to you.

Thank You

ACKNOWLEDGEMENTS

Thank you to the 500 leaders who were kind enough to share their wisdom and knowledge with me. This led to the creation of the High-Performance Team Model, a summary of what it takes to develop high-performance teams. I feel honoured to be able to pass on your experiences your expertise, and your passion.

I would also like to thank the following leaders for giving me deeper insights into their workplace, leadership style and challenges. Your ideas and experiences helped shape the case studies throughout the book.

Yiota Alexiadis	Marianne Marchesi
Toby Balazs	Olivia McMillan
Jay Claringbold	Louise Meadows
Katrina Dimitriu	Diana Nadebaum
Dominic Drenen	Stuart Pearce
Potta Findikidis	Kyle Redpath
Nick Hoare	Henry Ruiz
Daniel Le Roy	Nilesh Singh

A big thank you to the special people who helped me structure my thoughts and ideas into a book.

Lucie Bland

Jan Christian-Cage

Kylie Clarke

Andrew Mutton

Jo Sims

Finally, to my editor, Tanya Smith, whose valuable input and expert advice helped to refine my words and solidify my ideas.

REFERENCES

American Management Association. (2016). Retrieved from Does your team take responsiblity in the workplace: https://nevada-smallbusiness.com/does-your-team-take-responsibility-accountability-in-the-workplace/

Aon Hewitt. (2018). *https://www.kincentric.com/-/media/kincentric/pdfs/kincentric_2019_trends_global_employee_engagement.pdf*. Retrieved from Aon: https://www.kincentric.com/-/media/kincentric/pdfs/kincentric_2019_trends_global_employee_engagement.pdf

Aristotle. (340 BC). *Teachings*. Stagira: Self Published.

Bray, S. (2002). Role Efficacy, Role Clarity, and Role Performance Effectiveness. *Small Group Research*, 233-253.

Comcare. (2008). *Working Well: An organisational approach to preventing psychological injury*. Canberra: Comcare.

Erez, C. L. (2017). Does Rudeness Really Matter? The Effects of Rudeness on Task Performance and Helpfulness. *Academy of Management Journal*, No. 5.

EY Global. (2018). *Why business must harness the power of purpose*. Retrieved from https://www.ey.com/en_au/purpose/why-business-must-harness-the-power-of-purpose

Macquarie. (2017). *How to define your true business purpose*. Retrieved from Macquarie.com.au: https://www.macquarie.com.au/business-banking/how-to-define-your-true-business-purpose.html

Mankins, M. (2004). Stop Wasting Valuable Time. *Harvard Business Review*.

Maslow, A. H. (1943). A theory of human motivation. *Psychological review*.

Mental Health Commission of Canada, Calgary and Ottawa. (2012). *Psychological Health and Safety: An action guide for employers*. Canada: Mental Health Commission of Canada, Calgary and Ottawa.

Nurmesniemi, M. (2015). Workplace Accountability Study.

Nusca, A. (2018). *These Are Fortune's 100 Best Companies to Work For in 2018*. Retrieved from Fortune.

Partners In Leadership. (2014). *Workplace Accountability Study*. California: Partners In Leadership.

Phares, E. J. (1974). *Locus of control in personality*.

Porath, C. (2014). Half of Employees Don't Feel Respected by Their Bosses. *Havard Business Review*.

United States Office Of Personnel Management. (2015). *Performance Management*. Retrieved from OMP.GOV: https://www.opm.gov/policy-data-oversight/performance-management/reference-materials/more-topics/accountability-can-have-positive-results/

Walker, A. N. (2014). *The Examination of Organizational Respect in Relation to Organizational Culture*. New Hampshire: University of New Hampshire.

ABOUT THE AUTHOR

Rajiv is passionate about improving the business world—one leader at a time. With experience leading teams in senior roles across the banking, energy and technology sectors, and interviewing over 500 high-performance teams and leaders, Rajiv knows what it takes to create a high-performance team environment.

Rajiv combines real-world experience with evidenced-based coaching approaches as an International Coaching Federation certified coach to support leaders to maximise the potential of their teams through his company, Bare Coaching. He has worked with, guided and developed leaders in universities, technology firms, wine companies, start-ups and small businesses.

Rajiv lives in Melbourne, Australia and in his spare time loves spending time with his family and friends.

www.ingramcontent.com/pod-product-compliance
Lightning Source LLC
Chambersburg PA
CBHW060520090426
42735CB00011B/2308